WHEN
IT FEELS
LIKE THE
SKY IS
FALLING

WHEN IT FEELS LIKE THE SKY IS FALLING

H. NORMAN WRIGHT

HARVEST HOUSE PUBLISHERS
EUGENE, OREGON

When It Feels Like the Sky Is Falling

Copyright © 2018 H. Norman Wright
Published by Harvest House Publishers
Eugene, Oregon 97408
www.harvesthousepublishers.com

ISBN 978-0-7369-7484-4 (pbk.)
ISBN 978-0-7369-7485-1 (eBook)

Library of Congress Cataloging-in-Publication Data
Names: Wright, H. Norman, author.
Title: When it feels like the sky is falling / H. Norman Wright.
Description: Eugene : Harvest House Publishers, 2018.
Identifiers: LCCN 2018006853 (print) | LCCN 2018018023 (ebook) | ISBN 9780736974851 (ebook) | ISBN 9780736974844 (pbk.)
Subjects: LCSH: Suffering--Religious aspects--Christianity.
Classification: LCC BV4909 (ebook) | LCC BV4909 .W7595 2018 (print) | DDC 248.8/6--dc23
LC record available at https://lccn.loc.gov/2018006853

Contents

Introduction: Am I Really Safe?

If you are like most people, you want your life to be stable and predictable. Surprises and the unexpected tend to disrupt our lives.

Unexpected events or, as some prefer the *surprises of life*, are decisive times in your life. They are turning points for better or worse, for undesirable or positive outcomes. Some expected events can be anticipated, but many cannot. The unexpected carries a certain degree of risk or even uncertainty. We all experience the unexpected. But now we have a new fear in our country—terrorism. These acts are intensifying in frequency and destruction.

Terrorism has been with the world around us for centuries. Its roots and practices came from the first-century zealots. Finally, it's arrived on our shores. And so now our country as we know it has changed. It's been invaded, not by a foreign army or swarms of biologically altered insects, but by something that is more deadly: terrorism. Those who employ terrorism intentionally use violence to unsettle us. It doesn't take many of them to disrupt our daily lives, dominate our thinking, and take away our sense of safety. They strike where we least suspect their presence. They plant the seeds of suspicion, paranoia, and fear.

We tense up when we board a plane or walk through the doors of a subway train.

We wonder about things we never thought of ten years ago. The phrase *what if...* floods our mind.

When a terrorist attacks (and we can expect more), our lives are disrupted, not just for months, but for decades.

I've seen the results of terrorism and walked through the chaos. Never in my lifetime did I expect to walk through the rubble of Ground Zero, nor sit with the survivors of the shootings in Aurora, Colorado Springs, San Bernardino, or Las Vegas. But I have heard the survivors' stories. For some their life is changed forever.

LEARNING HOW TO RESPOND

This book is designed to help the reader handle the daily unexpected events and surprises as well as serious life-changing events. It will also help us handle and prepare for the present and future acts of terrorism. It will give practical and workable steps to use when an unexpected event occurs.

Whether the unexpected event was relatively minor or a devastating terrorist attack, no matter what happens, these kinds of occurrences share some common themes.

If the event was unexpected, the surprise element stuns and shocks. We feel dazed and disoriented. When the event is uncontrollable, and it's beyond our ability to change it, we feel powerless, vulnerable, and victimized.

Many events are unimaginable—the horrific elements are not familiar to our way of life. We have no frame of reference to make sense of what we witnessed. Many feel appalled and horrified. It's as if what was experienced was unreal. It was an event too strange to process. People saw but didn't comprehend what they were seeing, so the feelings of confusion and disorientation occur and intensify.

Some events, such as 9/11 and the various shootings that have happened in our country, seem unforgivable. The need to blame someone or something emerges. We wonder what we are to do with our anger, rage, and urge to punish. We feel powerless.

Since what occurred was unprecedented, there is no script to follow and so people feel directionless.

Almost all of us feel unprepared. After all, there's no reason to prepare ourselves for an unimaginable catastrophe. How *can* you prepare adequately? So defense mechanisms may be inadequate to handle the demand on our emotions. Overwhelmed is a common feeling.

Events such as what we talk about in this book leave a sense of uncertainty. We don't fully know the long-range effects on ourselves, our families, our jobs, our future, and the future of our children. There is a feeling of ambivalence and being torn between hope and fear.

The body and mind are overwhelmed. The faces of those who have been through trauma reflect the experiences above and beyond a person's ability to handle these events. I've sat with many survivors, and some of them will be described later in this book.

There are very few resources that address the unexpected or surprises, especially in the form of terrorism. That is why this book is desperately needed.

As you learn to become a resilient survivor in the daily events, you will be better able to handle the major upsets, including acts of terrorism.

A PERSONAL EXPERIENCE

The 41-year-old director of the American-Arab Anti-Discrimination Committee parked his car and headed for the building that housed his office. It was located in an upscale area of Orange County, California. The year was 1985, and terrorism had not yet reached the shores of our country, or so we thought.

This father of three small children usually brought his wife and youngest child with him to his office, but for some reason he left them home on this day. Twenty-one hours earlier he had appeared on a TV broadcast in which he criticized the media for some of their reporting. He also appeared as a pro-Arab spokesman on a CNN broadcast that was taped Thursday afternoon and had aired Thursday evening.

He took the stairs to his office on the second floor on Friday morning. He put his key into the lock, and as he opened the door, it triggered the release of an explosive device. The bomb went off, and the director suffered the full force of the blast. He was the first one in the office on that fateful day. His administrative assistant said she was the one who normally opened the office every morning, but Friday she was doing an errand for him before work. "He usually didn't come in until 10 or so," she said.

The man was taken by paramedics to Western Medical Center minutes after the 9:11 a.m. explosion, which blew out more than a dozen floor-to-ceiling windows in the building and showered the street below with glass, concrete, tattered drapes, and other debris. A hospital spokesman said he suffered severe injuries to his lower body and died at 11:24 a.m. after undergoing surgery.

Six employees of an insurance company across the hall from the committee offices in Santa Ana were treated for minor injuries at the same hospital and all were later released. Another woman who was either seated at a bus stop or walking in front of the building was also treated and later released from the hospital.

Offices on both sides of the damaged building, as well as an office across the street, were evacuated as deputies with the Orange County sheriff's bomb squad entered the building three times between 10:30 a.m. to 1:20 p.m., when the location was finally declared safe. The office manager in one of the adjacent offices in the building next door was asked by the authorities to vacate the premises for the day as a precaution.

One of those injured in the blast said, "I was just walking back to my desk when I heard a big explosion and saw the door fly open. We thought a heater blew up or something because there was so much smoke."

This employee said she was shaky and suffered from headaches. She said she did not remember at first how she got down from the second floor of the building. Later she recalled that a man from another building had helped clear the hallway of debris while she and the other occupants of the office walked out to the street. She and two co-workers then got in a car and drove themselves to the hospital.

Another person impacted said she was sitting at her desk when she "heard a loud noise, looked up, and saw the ceiling falling. The amount of smoke was overwhelming."

One individual who was attending a court reporting class across the street from the building where the blast occurred said, "I heard the explosion and ran to the window. Shards of glass were strewn across the street. I saw a man and a woman who were either standing in front of the building or had been sitting on the bench in front of it. They were trying to get away from the area. The woman looked like she was either going into shock or had sustained injuries."

There was no warning of a bombing in the Santa Ana case. This office had received threats and harassing calls, and employees had received calls at home by those threatening to kill them, but there had been no mention of a bomb. An FBI spokesman in Washington said that this agency had received thousands of threats every year.

That day I heard about the event, but I went about my daily activities as usual without giving too much thought to it. But that changed that evening when I was watching the news and saw the destruction the bomb had created. My eyes did not stay upon the destroyed office; they were drawn to the door of my own office. It was only a couple of hundred feet away from that building. My office manager had called earlier and said she had been asked to leave for the day, but she hadn't told me why. She worked for me in my counseling office, and one of the office buildings that authorities had closed was mine.

Slowly it began to dawn on me that someone had died and others were injured. If the bomb had been much larger, the devastation could have hit my office and those who were there on that day. Gradually the reality of this event began to penetrate as I sat and stared at the images on the screen. The thought *This doesn't happen to us* floated through my mind. But it did. No one is immune.

After all that was said and done, it was apparent that terrorism had gained a foothold in our country and was closer to home than I had imagined.

CHAPTER 1

Tremors in Our Life

What is it like to live with the unexpected? What events qualify as "unexpected"? I will share a number of unexpected experiences I have had that perhaps you can identify with. Personally, I would have rather missed out on some of them. But they are part of my life, and some shaped who I became.

One such event happened in 1952. It was unexpected. And it was slight. At first just a gentle sway. Then it stopped and everything was still. Silence. All of a sudden there was a sharp jolt and continuous movement that increased to the point that the bed and other furniture moved back and forth and up and down. We were in the middle of a major earthquake. All of Los Angeles felt the tremors. Damage here was slight. But not in Tehachapi and Bakersfield, 120 miles north of us—tremors there were intense. The ground shook, buildings crumbled, and lives were changed. It was totally unexpected.

Storms, earthquakes, tornados, accidents—these happen just in the lives of others…or do they? To describe these types of events I'll use the word *tremors*, for it might be the best descriptive word to convey what we experience. The word evokes numerous images and thoughts. We don't use the word very often. For some it's a negative image. It could be a warning that something is amiss or there's going to be a problem that needs attention.

Tremor—it's a word that doesn't denote stability, but just the opposite. What comes to mind is insecurity or shaking such as the ground does when an earthquake hits or it could be our hand as we age or when a physical disease begins to manifest itself. The dictionary describes it as "involuntary shaking of the body or limbs, as from disease, fear, weakness, or excitement; a fit of trembling. Any tremulous or vibratory movement; vibration: tremors following an earthquake."

All too often there is no warning. One moment we're stable and comfortable and the next we feel buffeted and overwhelmed. Some refer to this experience as having their life torn apart by a major storm. Others describe it as being blindsided.

Most people are exposed to at least one violent or life-threatening situation during the course of their lives. As people progress through the life cycle, they are also increasingly confronted with the deaths of close friends and relatives. Not everyone copes with these potentially disturbing events in the same way. Some people experience acute distress from which they are unable to recover. Others suffer less intensely and for a much shorter period of time. The more violent and unexpected, the more devastating.

None of us is immune to these events. Often they appear out of nowhere at the "wrong time," usually when it's most inconvenient. They disrupt our plans, and some leave devastation in their path. For some their experience is depicted in this way:

> In those few moments of realization, your focus changes from the everyday, ordinary issues of life, to the traumatic, catastrophic occurrences that make everything else seem miniscule. Your focus has been changed from the *mundane* to the *monumental.* Your feelings have escalated from *bland* to *ballistic* in a heartbeat. And while your heart is pounding, you hold your breath, and realization begins to sink into your consciousness. You've been blindsided and nothing will ever be the same again.[1]

Welcome to the world of the unexpected.

Often with these events we enter into a fog of disbelief. "No, this isn't happening, not to me—not now—not to us." For some this fog is impenetrable—a person can't make sense of this in their head.[2]

Some of these events are like fires. They start small in some unobserved area. If we see the smoke and catch the fire early, we can do damage control and avoid disastrous results. But left unobserved or unnoticed, the results could be long lasting and devastating.

Like you, I've experienced numerous tremors or events in my life. Some were slight and didn't affect my life, while others have been overwhelming and altered my life significantly. Each experience brought a mixture of responses and feelings, from upset, turmoil, and shock to a time of growth and change. Perhaps you will identify with some of these experiences.

In the early 1960s, I served on the staff of a church as a youth pastor and minister of education. Fresh out of seminary, I wasn't sure if I knew what to do. One of my first challenges revolved around the discovery that I would be serving more with the youth than with education. However, I made the adjustment and began to enjoy the ministry, and in time I saw some results. With 300 junior high, high school, and college students in my program, it was a busy time and full of unexpected events.

Each summer we took a group of high school students on an outreach or study outing. One year we took 25 of them to the High Sierras in Southern California, and for several days we camped in tents, hiked, fished, interacted, and studied. Nearby was a formidable, massive rock formation—Crystal Crag—over 1,000 feet high. At 10,364 feet, Crystal Crag is a dramatic and rugged mass of rock that is the recognizable landmark of the Mammoth Crest. The crag is a popular destination among mountaineers and climbers. The sheer wall was a challenge to even the most skilled climber.

But one morning two of the high school boys (one a recent graduate who was waiting to go into the navy) decided on their own to climb the face of this cliff. They left before others were awake and did not inform anyone of their plans. They probably knew we would have told them that the area was off-limits, since they were inexperienced and had no climbing gear. They walked the two miles to the base of the rock formation, made their way up the shale slide at the base of the rock, and proceeded to climb.

It's still unclear how they were able to scale the rock face given the lack of equipment and expertise, but they climbed for several hundred feet before Phil lost his handhold and plunged over 400 feet to his death. Every bone in his body was broken. His companion hung there watching in horror as his friend fell, but then he continued to climb until he was off the sheer wall and went for help. Hours later someone came to our camp and told us. There was a feeling of shock—disbelief—as we thought, *This isn't true*. A few minutes later, I watched a pack train walk by with Phil's body encased in a body bag hanging over the back of a horse. I watched until they were out of sight and then went to find a phone and call our senior pastor. It became his task to inform Phil's parents.

Did I know what to do at this time? Not really. Did I know what to say? No. Did I feel equipped to handle this event? Not at all. I had no preparation for anything like this. I think I felt like those in ministry in New York City following the 9/11 Twin Towers disaster. Most of them said, "I don't know what to say or do. I don't feel equipped." Neither did I. It was my first encounter with a combination crisis and traumatic event.

I'll never forget that day. We all sat in small groups talking in hushed voices, feeling numb and stunned. We fixed dinner, and then, strangely enough, our group began to joke, cut up, and laugh for the next hour. Other adults around us were bothered by their response. However, I realized later that this was their way of taking a break from the heaviness of the crisis. It was a normal response, because adolescents tend to move in and out of their grief more than adults do.

So, what would you have said or done? Would you have known how to respond? How would you have made sense of this tragedy? How do *you* respond when you're blindsided?

Often tremors are associated with disruptive weather patterns. These are often reflected in various storms. As unpredictable as some weather can be, we can usually tolerate it. But it's the storms of life that throw us.

Some storms are so new and different that we aren't sure what to do when they hit. This was brought home to me in a dramatic way when we experienced a tornado. Southern California, where my wife and I lived, is not known for having tornadoes. We have rain, Santa Ana winds, earthquakes, and hot weather, but no tornadoes…until a few years ago when a full-sized twister landed on our own street. I wasn't home, but my wife was.

While working in the yard, she began to feel some strange strong winds. Realizing that something was wrong, she went inside and shut the door. The winds continued, and it seemed as though the air was being sucked out of the house. She didn't know exactly what was happening, so she shut herself in one of the inner rooms.

About this time a neighbor turned the street corner and saw the twister touch down in the middle of the block and begin coming toward her. She drove her car into the garage and ran inside the house just before the tornado ripped a large tree from her front yard.

We were fortunate. No homes were lost, but several trees were uprooted. I guess the worst part was that this was trash day, and in front of each home were several full trash cans. After the tornado hit they were all empty! Everyone in our neighborhood was amazed, surprised, stunned. This just didn't happen in our area. No one knew what to do.

I remember another event that wasn't tied to the weather but was as devastating as a tornado.

I was standing on a field watching the participants of a cancer survivors' Relay for Life gathering. One of the survivors marching around the field was my wife, Joyce, since she was a cancer victim. As I watched, my cell phone rang, and I saw that it was a close friend I had known for almost 40 years. His first words were, "Norm, my son Matt is in heaven." I wasn't sure I had heard him right. "What? What did you say?" was my response. He replied again with the same words, "Matt is in heaven."

I felt stunned. Shocked. Not fully comprehending or believing what I had heard. No death notification is easy to accept, but especially not this one—a vibrant and quality 23-year-old young man with his sights set on graduate school and planning to marry in two months' time.

I'd known him since he was a boy, went fishing with him on many occasions, and had long conversations with him. I waited until after the Relay for Life event was over to share the news with my wife. A few weeks later, I flew back to the Midwest to be with my friend and his family.

It is through our dreams that meaning as well as delight are brought into our life. Meaning and delight are closely aligned with a sense of hope of something yet to come—something on the horizon that is better and more fulfilling, bringing a greater sense of meaning to our life. Some dreams, however, not only go unfulfilled or are altered, but they also are shattered and destroyed, and with them a portion of our life as well.

I saw this in the eyes and posture of the young man's father and in his siblings, his fiancée and her family, his grandparents, and his friends. Many times I heard this phrase or something similar expressed: "There's an empty place in my life, an immense hole, and it will never be filled in again." Events such as this take decades to overcome. These are tremors that continue to shake. Perhaps you've experienced this or know someone who has. Our sense of security, stability, and safety is shaken.

Over the years there have been many changes in my life and in some of my beliefs. The beliefs that life is fair, that bad things don't happen to good people, and that those who love the Lord are safe where we live and work have been challenged.

Over the past decade I've been involved in the aftermath and the process of recovery from numerous tragedies, including shootings, deaths, accidents, and bank robberies. One of the common responses I have heard and now expect to hear working with bank employees following a robbery is the statement, "It wasn't that they stole money from the bank. They also took away my feeling of safety. I can't feel safe here anymore." And that is what many experience after they have gone through a personal tremor.

For years I played racquetball two or three days a week. Now and then we played at a court a few miles away from Whittier, California. One morning we were in the middle of a game and I began to hear a low rumbling sound. It sounded as if the earth were growling. As it continued its sound and intensity increased, and I remember thinking, *That aerobics class on the floor above us is louder than usual.*

But as the sound continued, I realize two things: There was no aerobics class at this location, and the walls of the court were beginning to sway back and forth. They moved slowly and began to pick up momentum. It dawned on me: This was an earthquake, a large one. Then the lights dimmed and went out. Immediately we ran for the door. Not only was it dark, we couldn't open the door. In a racquetball court the door handles do not extend outward but are recessed so you don't run into them while playing. There we were, with a growing sense of panic and urgency, trying to find the handle without being able to see. Finally the door opened, and the building continued to shake while everyone ran outside (the quake hit while a number of individuals were changing or showering)!

We later learned the epicenter of this 5.9 quake (which damaged many structures and started multiple fires) was just seven miles away. Over 200 individuals were injured. There were eight fatalities. We were safe, but frightened. As I looked at the massive three-story garage adjoining the racquetball club, I decided not to park in the structure again. I would hate to be caught there if another massive quake occurred.

Earthquakes are like many events in our life. There is no warning. You can't predict them. They can either just rattle our lives or totally destroy our property or our life and its future.

Your tremor may come in the form of an event in the life of one of your family members.

The crises we experienced with our son were sometimes weekly or even daily. Matthew was born with what was labeled then as mental retardation and a gran mal seizure condition. But he was a loving child and changed our lives for the better. He lived with us until he was 11, and we then felt led to place him in a facility that could provide better care for him than we could. He never developed to be more than 18 months old mentally.

When he was 22, Matt developed reflux esophagitis and entered Loma Linda University Medical Center for corrective surgery.

The operation appeared to be successful, although the esophagus was thin as tissue paper from the erosion of stomach acids. It was torn during the surgery, but that was repaired. During the week of hospitalization, we were thankful for the competent doctors and nurses God had provided.

But in the first few days after surgery, Matthew suffered complications, and infection set in. We alternated staying at hotels near the hospital and driving home. After a week, additional surgery was performed. Following the second operation, Matthew stayed in the intensive care unit. He was heavily sedated and unconscious. There were eight tubes in him, and he was constantly on a ventilator. Unfortunately, he developed adult respiratory disorder syndrome. We were hopeful when the fever dropped and his blood pressure stabilized, but in several days we could see that he was not responding. The doctors felt he was in the Lord's hands. We prayed at his bedside for the Lord's will to be done.

We had stayed at our home the night of March 14 instead of at the motel near the Loma Linda hospital. On the morning of March 15 (the Ides of March), we had a call from the staff at the hospital. I heard the words, "You need to be here as soon as possible." A very generic phrase, but laden with meaning. We knew it was time.

We walked into the room, and the doctors told us that Matthew's lungs and heart were failing and would probably stop in about an hour. We felt helpless since there was nothing anyone could do to make Matthew well again.

We said good-bye to Matthew, and as we stood there, we saw Matthew's pulse rate decline ten beats. We stood almost traumatized, watching the change on the monitor and knowing what it meant.

His decreasing vital signs confirmed the reality that he was going to die soon, and within the hour Matthew died. The tremors of his passing continued for years and still do.

Losing one child is overwhelming. I never expected this loss to occur again. But it did. In May of 2015 I received a call that I can still hear in my mind as though it just occurred. "Norm, your daughter, Sheryl, died in the night." I heard, but I didn't hear. I heard, but it wouldn't register. My mind could not grasp the reality. It was as though a thousand-pound weight was pressing upon me. How could she die at fifty-three? It didn't make sense.

Death comes to us in many forms, bringing with it varying degrees of pain, sorrow, and grief. When it comes, it disrupts our life story, but no one experiences the disruption in the same way.

I wonder…I wonder, who are the loved ones you have lost? If this has not occurred yet to you, it will. You will enter the world of grief. It may be anticipated, or it can come as a sudden shock.

You, like many in our culture, will wonder if you are "doing grief" right. Death in our culture is an avoidant activity, as is the mourning process. Others may be more of a hindrance than a help. They will give you a time table for grief that is not appropriate. They may not know what to say and may wound you. They may say they know how you feel, but they don't really. If you express your grief in public, you won't be encouraged. Rather than validate your grief, they will try to help contain it.

A sudden death can make a shamble of schedules, priorities, agendas, and sometimes our most intimate relationships. A loved one's last breath inevitably changes us. The experience can be paralyzing, or it can be empowering. It can cause us to take life far more seriously.

We may feel anguish, wondering what the person's last moments were like, whether they were terrifying or painful. It is natural for their seconds or minutes of dying to become hours of emotional distress and lead to a crisis for us. Turning off thoughts of those moments our loved one experienced by sheer willpower alone is not easy and often it is impossible. Tremors cannot be contained, and we're at their mercy.

If you weren't there when the death occurred, this can also be a source of long-lasting regret. The fact that *no one* might have been there can also be stressful. Then you may have to deal with the painful mental process of second guessing; *if only* _____ had consulted a doctor earlier, and so on. Sudden deaths are often bizarre, like nightmares, because they are so unexpected. This is especially true of accidents.[3]

I serve as a hospital chaplain with the Victim Relief Chaplain organization. There are 15 of us, and we volunteer at the Kern Medical Center, which is the trauma unit for our county. We see or minister to some of the worst trauma cases. One evening we were asked to go to the ICU to meet with a patient and the nurses. The patient was being kept alive by machines, and there was no brain functioning. The family and nurses wanted us there while they disconnected the machines and allowed him to die. We prayed and read Scripture and then the medical staff shut off the machines.

Watching someone die can cause you to reflect on your own life. The other chaplain and I began to verbalize some questions that we don't usually discuss. I looked at my friend and said, "Have you ever thought about how you will die?" which led to other important but rarely asked questions. Some of which were prefaced by "What if…?"

There are many other questions that perhaps need to be asked. In keeping with the purpose of this book, one of the questions might be, "What is the worst thing that could happen to you?" Think about it for a while. We're all afraid of something—what is it for you? Aside from a physical illness, what is it? What is the worst unexpected event that you would give just about anything to avoid?

Is it possible to prepare for the unexpected? For some, but not all.

Is it possible to handle these kinds of events in a positive way? Yes, it is.

There's no way to prevent all catastrophes from happening, but that doesn't mean we can't prepare for them and minimize the losses. There are many situations that occur in life that we have been encouraged to prepare for. For example, our government has warned us to be prepared for numerous situations, but most of the time never told us why. As one person said, "It's as though we've been holding dress rehearsal for a play without knowing any of our lines."

Small upsets and tragedies can add up to major ones. Many of our disasters are predictable, but surviving them is not, and that's usually due to the lack of detailed preparation. It's important that we learn how we tend to respond to unexpected events. When something like this occurs, nothing is normal. We think and perceive differently. We become superheroes with learning disabilities. We are seen as strong, but are not able to live up to what we appear to be. At this time, many, if not most, people tend to shut down entirely in a disaster, quite the opposite of panicking. They go slack and seem to lose all awareness.[4]

Others are what we call *silent screamers.*

So…is it possible to overcome these events rather than let these events overcome us? Again, there is a "yes" answer. And that's what this book is all about.

My journey into the field of the unexpected was like watching a number of threads come together to form a single tapestry. As a Christian counselor, I spent hours sitting and listening to the stories of broken lives, broken marriages, and broken souls. Over the years of listening to these stories, I always said to myself, "Yes, I hear your story, my friend, but there's something else in there. There's more to this story." Whether they could articulate it or not, underneath the brokenness of their lives, nearly every person who came to me for counseling had a story of the unexpected. And every trauma story contained the profound and soul-shattering wounds of loss and grief.

I knew these stories of a past trauma were still fueling their pain in the present. The trauma from the past haunted and controlled their lives. For example, a young woman came to see me whose life was shaken and traumatized years earlier by a bone-jarring, building-toppling earthquake that was her unexpected loss. Even many years later, when she finally came to see me for counseling, she still couldn't open a newspaper for fear that it might trigger some painful memories.

As a seminary professor, I also met numerous young men who had come back from the Vietnam War, still shaken, still suffering from PTSD (post-traumatic stress disorder). These stories of past trauma were legion. Everywhere I turned I seemed to hear stories about the lingering effects of the unexpected and unthinkable. Each story represented only a single thread, but the threads were definitely weaving a larger picture.

People who have experienced these kinds of events know firsthand one of the sad truths about life: Most people don't know how to deal with the unexpected. It's a strange and even terrifying topic for discussion. So we pretend that it doesn't exist or that it will go away. But the effects never just go away.

So I found my story of loss intersecting with the stories of many who had experienced trauma and loss. As I walked beside my fellow sufferers, they hungered to process the pain—if only someone would listen. I began to see the world through the eyes of the hurting and traumatized. For instance, I started to hurt for the four out of ten servicemen and women serving in Iraq who returned home still suffering from the effects of post-traumatic stress disorder. As I counseled the survivors of 9/11, I also realized that this event had traumatized so many people in the country who lost loved ones or even just watched the coverage on television. I especially thought of the children whose innocence was shattered by the vivid scenes from that horrible day.

Because the theme of trauma has cut so deeply into my life, I often find myself viewing the world through a unique lens—the lens of trauma. Such a lens helps one to see what others might not see.

A few years ago I was watching a television show that was interrupted by a live news report about an enraged man on a Los Angeles freeway. As the news cameras rolled, thousands of people watched in horror as this man waved a Molotov cocktail in the air and threatened to kill himself on live television. Like everyone watching that day, I prayed and hoped for a peaceful solution. But I also said out loud (as if the reporters could hear me), "Cut the tape! This man is going to blow himself to bits, and thousands of people, including hundreds of children, will have a scene of graphic violence etched on their minds for years to come. Please have some sense to turn off the cameras." Unfortunately, they didn't.

A trip to hurricane-ravaged New Orleans served to reinforce and deepen this commitment to view the world through the lens of trauma. On October 17, 2005, I landed in Baton Rouge to help with the Victim Chaplain Ministry. I wasn't prepared for what I encountered. What you and I saw in the media could never capture the reality of this event. There are no words to describe the devastation I saw in New Orleans. It was one thing to hear that 80 percent of the city was under water, but it was another to drive mile after mile, the only vehicle on side streets, and see nothing but crushed, shattered, and empty homes. From the poorest tiny structure to the expensive mansion, no house could withstand the force of Hurricane Katrina. Whatever wasn't flattened was torn and twisted. I saw large boats hundreds of yards inland, heavy pianos hanging out of windows, and cars standing on end or perched on top of walls.

For most residents in the Ninth Ward (or the ghetto, as it is often described), there was nothing to return to. The homes there and even miles away would need to be bulldozed. Wood furnishings as well as the soil were contaminated. There was nothing to restore or rebuild. It would take at least five years or longer to reconstruct. And where did one begin? It was overwhelming.

One elderly woman, very upset and anxious over her losses, was invited to rest in our motor home while a worker went to where her home used to be and searched through the pile. The only personal item he could find was a picture frame, which she clutched in her arms. She was still holding on to it when she left, for it was the only possession that remained after 60 or 70 years of living there.

The deepest traumas involved the loss of loved ones. I listened to a conversation in which a middle-aged man called wanting to find his nine-year-old daughter, who he knew was dead. He was holding her hand as he climbed into the attic, but she slipped from his grasp and he never saw her again. She was afflicted with cerebral palsy and was partially disabled. To speed up the identification process, he shared that she had a hip transplant with a titanium part.

If a family member's body was found, the funeral rituals of their culture had been lost, for friends and other family members had been relocated. There would be no marching with musicians, no pastor or church or support for their grief.

This past month I sat with those whose lives have changed forever because of what had happened in Las Vegas. It was November first, and for many there would be an empty chair at the

Thanksgiving table as well as at Christmas. A well-known family in my city would be missing their 20-year-old daughter. The shooter's bullet had taken her life as she tried to run to safety. Hundreds came to the service to pay tribute as well as to support the family.

There was a group of high school students sitting in stunned silence upon hearing that their teacher would never walk into their room again. She didn't make it to safety as she desperately tried to get out of harm's way. She couldn't outrun the bullets even though she ran so fast trying to find a place to hide.

I heard the sorrow in a wife's voice as she described how her husband had tried to cover and protect her as she lay on the ground with bullets ricocheting off the ground and fragments bouncing around. Her voice cracked and became hesitant as she said someone had moved his body and they had searched for it for hours but didn't know who took him and where he was now. She was still searching for answers even after she found her husband in the morgue of a hospital.

These incidents changed the lives of hundreds and will continue to impact thoughts, beliefs, feelings, and decisions for years to come. The tragic unexpected events have a power and domination not just on a few but on a multitude.

Have you ever taken a raft trip? Many of us have. Rivers have numbers attached to them to identify the intensity of the flow of the water. Rapids are classified by a Class I to Class VI rating.

Class I is easy, with fast-moving water with riffles and small waves. Risk is slight.

Class VI is extreme and extraordinarily difficult, and runs of this classification are rarely attempted. They are difficult, unpredictable, and dangerous. They are for experts only.

In some rivers, you can float along at a leisurely pace; the water is calm. You can see the logs and boulders, and there is a gentle sway to the raft or boat. But other rivers are known for their white water. The river is full of turbulence, and it's difficult to know where the submerged rocks and logs are. If you take one of those white-water trips, you can expect to get dumped out of the raft and into the water at some point. You're prepared for it, expect it, and handle it when it happens.

Life is full of uncharted waters. Those who adapt, those who can be flexible, handle the turbulence better than others and are able to get back in the raft at some time.[5]

We can resist change or the unexpected or go with it and adapt.

> Resisting change wears down our bodies, taxes our minds and deflates our spirits. We keep doing the things that have always worked before with depressingly diminishing results. We expend precious energy looking around for someone to blame—ourselves, another person, or the world. We worry obsessively. We get stuck in the past, lost in bitterness or anger. Or we fall into denial—*everything's fine. I don't have to do anything different.* Or magical thinking—*something or someone will come along to rescue me from having to change.* We don't want to leave the cozy comfort of the known and familiar for the scary wilderness of that which we've never experienced. And so we rail against it and stay stuck.[6]

Fill out the following chart.

The 10 Worst Unexpected Events That Could Happen to Me

Situation	What I could do?
1.	
2.	
3.	
4.	

Situation	What I could do?
5.	
6.	
7.	
8.	
9.	
10.	

What's the likelihood that these things could happen to you? On a scale of 0–10, attempt to evaluate the likelihood: 10 would be it's certain, whereas 0 would be not at all.

One author suggested the following:

> Let's assume you've assumed the worst. Now, how likely is it that the crisis that you have just envisioned for yourself will ever affect this event?
>
> Is there a "slim chance" that it could happen?
>
> How about a "once in a blue moon" chance?
>
> Or would you call the odds "pretty good"?[7]

Have you heard the term *damage estimate*? If there is a good likelihood of this event occurring, it may be best to determine before it hits what to do if it did occur, especially if you can't stop it, avert it, control it, or abort it. It's best to do a damage estimate before the event happens. For example, in California where I live, most of us carry earthquake insurance. In other sections of the country many carry flood insurance. Many have thought, *This really won't happen to me*, but are you sure it won't?[8]

One last thought—when we experience the unexpected, our life and our plans are interrupted. We resist this. We don't like it or want it. Could it be that this was not a surprise but rather an intervention; not an accident, but allowed? An intervention by God? He has a purpose that isn't yet revealed. It will unfold in time. It's something to think about; as are these scriptures:

> "For I know the plans I have for you," declares the LORD, "plans to prosper you and not to harm you, plans to give you hope and a future" (Jeremiah 29:11).
>
> Call to me and I will answer you and tell you great and unsearchable things you do not know (Jeremiah 33:3).

You see, life is full of the unexpected, the unthinkable, the predictable, and the unpredictable. If we understand this fact, we will be able to handle the storms and surprises that drop into our lives from time to time.

When we're hit by these events, we're thrown off course and often go into a tailspin like a plane that has lost its power. Is it possible to prevent or bypass these events of life? No. Is it possible to survive them and even grow stronger because of them? Yes. And that's what this book is about. It's not just surviving, but about learning to let God use these events in your life to make you stronger in your dependence on Him.

Oh, you'll cry out and ask the question "Why?" We all do. It's often our initial response. But in time, our cry of protest will change as we understand the meaning of our pain and suffering.

I wrote this book to help you to understand the meaning of life's events so you can truly be a survivor. It *is* possible to rebound when life's storms knock you down.[9]

CHAPTER 2

The Unexpected—Inevitable

What would you call these events we are talking about? We have different names for them: intruders, surprises, the unexpected, stresses, uncharted waters, spoilers, changes, or even crises. What are they specifically? How do you know when you're in crisis? Let's use this word since we're familiar with it. It's used all the time, and a number of events labeled as crises are the typical everyday variety.

Several elements work together to make up this disruptive condition. When you're aware of the four phases or stages and understand how they contribute to what you're experiencing, you can take the first step toward handling these experiences in a more positive manner and becoming a survivor.

The first phase is usually some *sudden unexpected upsetting event*. All these words are important. This can be anything that starts a chain reaction of events, which in turn leads to a crisis. It could be something that seems minor or life threatening. For example:

- A young wife who prepared for her career for seven years now discovers she is unexpectedly pregnant.

- A college senior who gave himself to basketball during school in order to play in the professional basketball association shatters an ankle while hiking.

- A manager of a small company is severely hurt by a bomb set off in the subway.

- A widower who is raising five preadolescent children loses his job in a very specialized profession.

- Your bank is robbed while you are there.

- A gunman comes to your school and opens fire.

- You live in the southern states and Hurricane Irma came for a visit with total devastation.

- A wildfire erupted and you don't know if your home survived or not.

What these people have in common is an event that disrupts their life at this time.

Whenever you find yourself getting upset or having difficulty coping, ask yourself, "What event is occurring or has just occurred in my life?" The cause of your upset is usually fairly obvious to you or others. But if you can't identify it, ask for help. It may be more obvious to someone else.

The second element contributing to this state is *your vulnerability.* Not all negative events lead to a crisis. You have to be vulnerable in some way for an event to become a crisis. For example, if you go without sleep for a couple of nights, you could be vulnerable to a situation you usually handle without difficulty. But this could also be an event that threatens your safety or your life. Your past impacts you more than you realize. Illness or depression lowers a person's coping ability, as do unresolved emotional issues from the past. Consider whether you relate to any of these:

> The hurts of the past keep us from the joy of the present and the future.

The baggage of the past can be summed up in one word: *hurt*. It could be physical, mental, emotional, or spiritual.

The word *denial* is overused and probably misused as well. But many of us were taught to deny our feelings. We also deny them because at the time of our trauma or hurt, we needed denial to help us cope.

We learn to tune the pain and hurt out like adolescents tune out parental lecture.

When you numb one emotion, you numb them all. When you flush away your bad feelings, the good ones go down the drain too.

Many of us have pasts so wracked with pain that our pattern of life is devoted to playing it safe, and thus not run the risk of being hurt again. We find ways to create a safe distance and avoid losses, as well as build walls to keep others out.[1]

The problem is what we buried in the past intensifies the present upset. (For more information and details on the past see my book *When the Past Won't Let You Go* [Eugene, OR: Harvest House, 2016].)

Recently I talked with a woman who wanted to give up her foster child, cancel an important fund-raising event, and quit her business. Why? Because she was depressed over the threat of another loss in her life. She was overwhelmed and felt like giving up everything! I asked her not to make any life-changing decisions during her time of depression because she might regret those decisions later. And these were major changes that would impact her and her family.

I've talked to several people recently who were present at the shooting in Las Vegas. They are hesitant to go out in public because of the crowds of people as well as the sounds that remind them of the event.

The third phase in a crisis is *the actual upset.* You know, the last straw! These are the times when you seem to cope with one upsetting event after another, then go to pieces when you drop a piece of food on your clothes. In reality, your reaction to dropping the food is a reaction to all the other events. It's like saving up all your upsets and dumping the whole load on a family member who does something you don't like. Out comes all the accumulated anger at once. Most, if not all, the anger is about things completely unrelated to what your family member just did.

The last phase is *the actual state of crisis.* Everyone differs in the way they handle this. A crisis is often an everchanging, unstable situation, somewhat like an illness. With an illness you have to identify what it is and then take care of yourself. The key word is *identify,* which has to happen before you can deal with the crisis.

If I were to ask you how you respond to crisis, what would you say? When you feel that you can no longer handle what is happening in your life, then it becomes a crisis.

Usually there are actual symptoms of stress, which include physiological or psychological factors, or both. These symptoms can include depression, anxiety, headaches, bleeding ulcers, and more. In other words, you experience some type of extreme discomfort. I've talked to a number of those from the Las Vegas shooting and as they talk their bodies tremble.

You also experience a sense of panic or defeat. You may feel as though you've tried everything and nothing works. You feel like a failure; you feel defeated, overwhelmed, helpless. Hope? There is no hope.

At this point you can respond in one of two ways: One way is to become agitated and engage in behavior that is counterproductive—pacing back and forth, taking drugs, driving too fast, getting into arguments or fights. The other is to become apathetic, which is equally counterproductive. This could include excessive sleeping or drinking or the use of drugs to the extent that you no longer feel the pain.

Your main concern at this point is getting relief. We look for an escape from the pain of stress. And we want it now—instead of later; we want God to respond to our prayers and change our situation.

In a major crisis we're not usually in a condition to solve our problems in a normal manner. This adds to our state of confusion, since we're usually capable of functioning quite well. Shock makes a person appear dazed and respond in bizarre ways. If you're in shock, you may feel frantic and look to other people for help. In fact, you may become overly dependent upon others to help you out of the dilemma.

This is also a time of decreased efficiency. You may continue to function normally, but instead of responding at 100 percent capacity, your response may be at 60 percent. This, too, disturbs you. The greater the threat from your own appraisal of what's happening, the less ability you'll have to cope.

When I work with groups or individuals, I warn them that their thinking ability at this time is limited. They won't remember as well or be as sharp. They also need to watch their driving since this is a time when they are most likely to get a ticket or have an accident. Often after I say this or before I can finish, someone raises a hand and says, "You're too late, Norm. I got a ticket on the way over here," or "I was driving and I missed the turnoff."

I worked with a group of high school students who witnessed a classmate being shot in front of them in their classroom. One student said, "Norm, prior to the shooting I had all the information for my class memorized. I knew it frontward and backward. I could ace the exam. Now I can't remember anything!"

Is it possible to avoid experiencing a crisis? Yes and no, for upsets and surprises are a part of life. Also, some situations are true crises; others are problems that escalate into crisis.

There are three factors that affect the intensity of what you are experiencing and may contribute to an event becoming a crisis. They are how you view a problem, how much support you have from others, and how strong your coping mechanisms are. These are significant.

First, let's talk about the way you view a problem and the meaning it has for you. Some events would be threatening for anyone, whereas some may be threatening *just for you*. Sometimes your perception makes the event threatening. Your beliefs, ideas, expectations, and perceptions all work together to determine how you see what is happening as well as the outcome.

We have our own way of perceiving an event. If a friend responds to a certain event more intensely than you do, it probably has more meaning for them than it does for you.

Two people can view the same event differently, depending on several factors. For instance, you appraise the death of a close friend from several viewpoints: how close the relationship was, how often you were in touch with that friend, how you have responded to other losses, and how many losses you have experienced recently. A woman deeply involved in her husband's life perceives his death differently than does a close friend, a business associate, or the uncle who saw the deceased once every five years.

When you experience a crisis, you're perceiving the loss or threatened loss of something important to you. Think of what is most important to you. Is there anything in your life right now in danger of turning into a crisis? If you're having trouble formulating an answer, perhaps the following scenario can help you discover what is most important to you in your home:

> You've been informed that your house is going to be completely destroyed in a few minutes. You have time to make one trip out of your home, taking with you what is most important and valuable to you. What will you take?

No matter what you say you'll take, you won't unless you plan, because it's a crisis and you won't remember. You can't think.

But if you make a list and post it, you will remember (yes, I have a posted list!).

People are often surprised at what has meaning for them and what doesn't. This exercise also causes some people to reevaluate what they feel is important.

Consider another scenario:

> What event, if it were to occur in the next twelve months, would be the most upsetting or devastating to you? List four more events in order of importance, using the same criteria. Now think about how you would handle these events and work through the loss involved in each one. (You may want to return to the first chapter.)

A second factor that affects the intensity of a crisis is whether or not we have an adequate network of friends, relatives, or agencies to support us. This is where the body of Christ should come into play as one of the greatest support groups available. But the church needs to know how to respond at such a time. I know of several churches that respond to a person's or family's loss of a loved one by having a different family assigned to minister to them every week for a year. They call the family, send notes, deliver food, take them out, and so on. Since the shootings in Las Vegas and Sutherland, Texas, many people are coming forward to support the survivors and will be doing this not for days, but for months and years.

A third factor that helps determine whether an event becomes a crisis or not involves a person's coping mechanism. If your coping skills and abilities don't function well, or they break down quickly, then you may be overwhelmed. Some coping mechanisms are healthy while others are destructive. Coping mechanisms run the gamut—rationalization, denial, researching what others do, praying, reading Scripture, and more. The greater the number and diversity of *healthy* coping methods you employ, the less likely it is that a problem or upset will overwhelm you.

HOW PEOPLE RESPOND TO A CRISIS

When you experience a crisis, your response may differ from that of family members or friends. However, there are some basic responses common to most people, depending on what comforts them during difficult times. Take a look at some typical responses and see if you can identify how you respond:

- Some look for others to protect and control them at a time of crisis. They say, "Please take over for me."

- Some need a person who will help them maintain contact with what is reality and what isn't. They say, "Help me know what's real at this time. Let me know what's true and what isn't."

- Some feel terribly empty and need loving contact with others. They say, "Care for me, love me."

- Some need another person to be available at all times in order to feel secure. They say, "Always be there. Never leave."

- Some have an urgent need to talk. They say, "Let me get this off my chest. Listen to me tell the story again and again."

- Some need advice on certain pressing matters. They say, "Tell me what to do."

- Some need to sort out their conflicting thoughts. They say, "Help me put things into perspective."

- Some need the assistance of some type of specialist. They say, "I need some professional advice."

Perhaps you identify with some of these responses. If so, it may help to share your need with those closest to you.

Why do some seem to handle these events well while others don't? Consider some characteristics of those who appear to have the most difficulty handling crisis.

Some are just *emotionally fragile* to begin with, and specific events are more difficult for them to handle.

Those who have a *physical ailment* or *illness* will struggle because of fewer resources upon which to draw.

Those who *deny reality* have a hard time coping with a crisis. Some may deny the fact that they're seriously ill or financially ruined or that their child is on drugs or that they have a terminal illness.

When the unexpected occurs, some regress into self-medication through their mouth. They feel uncomfortable unless they're doing something with their mouth, such as eating, talking, or smoking. This *refusal to face the real problem* can continue for some time and can actually help to create an additional problem for the person. And it can push others away.

Another characteristic is an *unrealistic approach to time.* Some people crowd the time dimensions of a problem or they extend the time factors way into the future. They want the problem to be "fixed" right away or they delay addressing it. To rush may mean not addressing the problem adequately. To delay avoids the discomfort of reality but enlarges the problem.

Those who struggle with *excessive guilt* will have difficulty coping with a crisis. They tend to blame themselves for the difficulty, which increases feelings of guilt, which further immobilizes them. Many struggle with survivor guilt.

Another characteristic of those who do not cope well with crisis is the tendency to be *overly dependent* or *overly independent.* Such people either turn down offers of help or become clinging vines. Those who cling suffocate you if you're involved in helping them. Overly independent people refuse offers of help. They don't cry out for help, even if they're sliding down the hill toward disaster. When the disaster hits, they either continue to deny it or blame others for its occurrence.

Dr. Amanda Ripley has given us several suggestions on how to boost your survival odds and work on building resilience. Many have suggested that attitude makes a difference. Those who do well in a crisis and recover tend to have some beliefs and advantages:

- They believe they can influence what happens to them.
- They find meaningful purpose in life's turmoil.
- They are convinced they can learn from both good and bad.

Their focus is basically positive potential, and practice makes a definite difference. Resilience can be built through rehearsal—practicing positive steps over and over again does make a difference.

Even talking to yourself differently with phrases such as "I can handle this" or "I will recover" again and again has an impact on your brain. Tell yourself there is meaningful purpose here, and repeat over and over that you can learn from this ordeal. Even if you don't entirely believe it, your brain is listening.

Another principle that makes a difference is building relationships with your neighbors. Most of us don't know those who live more than one or two houses away unless we all have children of similar age.

A third suggestion is lowering anxiety, worry, and fear. Those with higher anxiety, worry, and fear levels may have a greater tendency to overreach or misread danger signs. They're on alert or more vigilant than others.

A fourth is to identify your risk in advance and evaluate whether it is real or not.

Finally, train your brain by practicing what you would do in the event of an earthquake, shooter, fire, etc. This will impact performance.[2]

YOUR PERCEPTION OF GOD

There is another factor to consider that has bearing on all the others—*how you perceive God.* The belief in God and how we perceive Him is a reflection of our theology, yet so many people are frightened by it.

Many times when we go through difficult upsets and crises we're forced to evaluate what we truly believe. Unfortunately, many determine what they believe by what they are going through. They allow their theology to be determined by their circumstances. When they hit the problems of life, they seem to negate the promises of God and begin to wonder if He cares!

Sometimes crisis changes our view of God. Max Lucado describes the process well:

> There is a window in your heart through which you can see God. Once upon a time that window was clear. Your view of God was crisp. You could see God as vividly as you could see a gentle valley or hillside. The glass was clean the pane unbroken.
>
> You knew God. You knew how he worked. You knew what he wanted you to do. No surprises. Nothing unexpected. You knew that God had a will, and you continually discovered what it was.
>
> Then, suddenly, the window cracked. A pebble broke the window. A pebble of pain.
>
> Perhaps the stone struck when you were a child and a parent left home—forever. Maybe the rock hit in adolescence when your heart was broken. Maybe you made it into adulthood before the window was cracked. But then the pebble came.
>
> Was it a phone call? "We have your daughter at the station, you better come down here."
>
> Was it a letter on the kitchen table? "I've left. Don't try to reach me. Don't try to call me. It's over. I just don't love you anymore."

Was it a diagnosis from the doctor? "I'm afraid our news is not very good."

Was it a telegram? "We regret to inform you that your son is missing in action."[3]

Why do we end up feeling disappointed by God? Is it really because of Him, or could it be because of our own expectations? We have our own unexpressed agenda. We believe, "If God is God, then..." But does our agenda match the teaching of Scripture? Those who believe in the sovereignty and caring nature of God have a better basis upon which to approach life.

Dr. Robert Hicks had some insights about the presence of God.

The first step in healing from our psychic pain is to recognize that God was really present when the tragedy occurred. Even though you may feel that He was absent, He was very much there, grieving, hurting, and perhaps even being angered by the injustice of it. God does not lead a sheltered life, as some think. His universal presence extends to the worst of events. God was in Vietnam; He was at the Holocaust; He was at the rape scene; He was there when a child died. He is still here. We cannot flee from His presence even when we try. As one griever told me, "I found that I ran right into Him when I was running away." Healing begins in His presence. It is in His presence that new reconstructive emotions (joy and pleasure) have their origins (see Psalm 16:11). These emotions must come from the conviction that Someone cares deeply about me and knows exactly what I have experienced because He was there in the trauma. In this sense, the first thing we can do for our healing is to return to God.[4]

A book that has spoken to me every time I've read it is Lewis Smedes' *How Can It Be All Right When Everything Is All Wrong?* He has been through life's tough times. His insights and sensitivity to crises and God's presence and involvement in our lives can answer many of our questions. One of his personal experiences shows how our theology helps us through life's changes.

The other night, trying to sleep, I amused myself by trying to recall the most happy moments of my life. I let my mind skip and dance where it was led. I thought of leaping down from a rafter in a barn, down into a deep loft of sweet, newly mown hay. That was a superbly happy moment. Yet somehow my mind was also seduced to a scene some years ago that, as I recall it, must have been the most painful of my life. Our firstborn child was torn from our hands by what felt to me like a capricious deity I did not want to call God. I felt ripped off by a cosmic con-artist. And for a little while, I thought I might not easily ever smile again.

But then, I do not know how, in some miraculous shift in my perspective, a strange and inexpressible sense came to me that my life, our lives were still good, that life is good because it is *given*, and that its possibilities were still incalculable. Down into the gaps of feeling left over from the pain came a sense of givenness that nothing explains. It can only be felt as a gift of grace. An irrepressible impulse of blessing came from my heart to God for his sweet gift. And that was joy…in spite of pain. Looking back, it seems to me now that I have never again known so sharp, so severe, so saving a sense of gratitude and so deep a joy, or so honest.[5]

A NEEDED OUTLET

The feelings you experience in a crisis come as waves. The earthquake intensity of any crisis recedes, and then the tidal waves of emotions begin their hammering process. And they keep rolling in, wave after wave.

These feelings have to have an outlet. If not, they won't stay buried. One day they will explode with a vengeance. One author describes it well.

I will never forget the time my dad left a can of aerosol spray in the back window of the family car while he was playing golf. The sun pounded on the window for a couple of hours and then the can detonated, shattering the windows and slicing a hole in the steel roof of the car. The force was unimaginable.

It's the same with unexpressed feelings born in the midst of crisis. They fester and fester until they explode, adding damage to damage, doing nothing to reduce the problem.[6]

Perhaps this chapter has been reflective of some of your life experiences. Perhaps you've walked through a problem that turned into a crisis and you now understand what factors led up to it and what intensified it. Or it could be that this chapter was a window into the future for you, since your crises have yet to hit. They will.

It's true, the unexpected will either destroy us or transform us. Isn't it sad that the first lesson most of us learn about crisis is when we experience it? Why weren't we taught about the reality of crisis and its characteristics, and how to be prepared to handle crises, before they hit?

Survivors—those with *resilience*—are the people who understand the meaning of these events, the typical ways of responding to a crisis, and the stages a person will experience as he or she walks through it. As you read the next chapter you will realize that what you've experienced in your crisis times is normal. This knowledge not only brings a sense of relief but provides help in becoming a person of resilience.

CHAPTER 3

Colorado Springs

The following is just one experience of terror and healing. Unfortunately, there will be more of these in our future.

Three of us were asked to minister in 2007 at a large church in which hundreds were traumatized by a gunman. I've included this story since situations such as this are becoming more frequent. This also occurred within weeks following the death of my wife of 48 years. This story was written immediately following our ministry to this church.

> The Lord is my rock, my fortress and my deliverer;
>   my God is my rock, in whom I take refuge;
>   my shield and the horn of my salvation, my
>   stronghold.
> I called to the Lord, who is worthy of praise,
>   and I have been saved from my enemies...
> He rescued me from my powerful enemy,
>   from my foes, who were too strong for me.
> They confronted me in the day of my disaster,
>   but the Lord was my support (Psalm 18:2-3,17-18).

THE INCIDENT

A lone gunman shot four young missionaries with YWAM (Youth with a Mission) at a church in Denver, killing two of them, and then drove to a church in an adjacent town. This was a very prominent church. Apparently the gunman had been expelled from YWAM in the past and at one time had a confrontation with two staff members at the church in the other town.

The gunman arrived at the church, then waited until 1:00 p.m., until most of the security guards had left. He placed two smoke bombs in strategic places, drove to another entrance to the church, and exited his car. He had two semiautomatic hand guns, a semi-automatic assault rifle, and 1,000 rounds of ammunition. For more than a year he had amassed these weapons. He first opened fire on a van in which there was a family of six. The 18- and 16-year-old daughters were killed (one died instantly and the other died following surgery), and the father was shot twice in the abdomen. In the car there were also a 12-year-old, the 18-year-old's twin sister, and the mother.

He then opened fire on another vehicle, hitting it with seven or eight rounds and wounding the mother through the shoulder. He shot through the doors of the church, then entered the hallway, shooting as he went, where he was confronted by a female security guard who shot him. It appears now that her shots dropped him and he then shot himself in the head.

THE RESPONSE

Our chaplain ministry was asked to respond and assist the congregation and pastors. We were called there to conduct debriefings, engage in counseling, teach, provide help and support to the staff and congregation, and basically minister in any way we could. And we did. It was demanding, fulfilling, and exhausting. We ministered but came away feeling we were ministered to by the congregation and staff. This was a caring, concerned, and loving congregation who sought as much help as they could receive. It was also a praying congregation, and this was quite obvious. We were impressed by how this church responded within the initial 48 hours. Story after story was told on how God guided and intervened during the minutes of terror. Since this event occurred following the second service, there were thousands who had already left the premises. But between 300 to 500 people were involved in some way during or after the shooting. Some saw bodies or the shooter and some heard shots.

The first morning we went to the hospital to meet with the family who had lost two children. This was a close-knit family who lived in Denver but were very involved in ministry at this church. From the time they were taken from the church to the hospital they were surrounded by several pastors who were constantly praying for them.

Upon arriving we learned that the mother and daughters were scheduled to visit the funeral home to view the bodies, but the mother wasn't ready and was under sedation. The mother sat in a chair of the hospital room with a blanket wrapped around her. Later she opened her eyes and said, "I'm concerned about my sisters who are here. They're so angry over this. I have several siblings, and over 30 years ago our mother was burned. This has brought all that back again since we never really faced it. They need to talk to someone." I sought them out and we talked for a while.

Then I went into the father's room and listened to his story. His response was a mixture of intense grief and sorrow as well as hope for the future. His faith and dependence upon the Lord was amazing. There was still a sense of numbness in the family's response, and their future will be very painful but will be sustained by their faith. The two daughters who were killed had just returned from a mission trip to China. Their father made a significant observation when he said, "We were a family of six, but now we will have to reconfigure since there are only four left. We don't have two to respond to, or play off of, and we will need to learn new ways to respond."

The surviving 18-year-old twin was there with her boyfriend, and upon meeting his parents, who were caring for the two remaining daughters, I discovered they were Biola University graduates and the father had attended Talbot Seminary for a while.

The next day the medical staff put a 24-hour lockdown on the family. They had been telling their story so much it was overwhelming them and now they were unable to even finish their sentences. They needed rest. Hopefully in future situations that others will experience, someone will be available to write the story on behalf of the victims and then distribute it to personnel who need the information. At such an early stage in a victim's experience, repetitively telling the story simply reinforces the trauma.

What's more, the mother was determined to go to the funeral home with two of her sisters and shampoo and comb the girls' hair in preparation for the memorial service. We were very concerned about the possible re-traumatization that this may cause in spite of the help it might be for the mother.

Later on I went to the church for the first of three large group sessions. The initial meeting was with the staff of about 100 with an additional 50 college interns. We met for an hour and a half, and every meeting that day had to be uniquely adapted and crafted. It was a mixture of debriefing, teaching about grief, crisis, and trauma, as well as giving meaning and hope based on the Scripture. The following is what I said for the introductory remarks after they had shared their own story with one another:

"Thank you for coming here to this meeting. Some of you probably wish you were elsewhere and the purpose of this gathering wasn't necessary. And especially at this time of year we shouldn't have to be here because of a tragedy. For this is the season of wishes experienced and wishes fulfilled. We wish and hope for enjoyable family experiences and we wish for certain presents. But in the midst of this significant season, there has been a deadly intrusion into our lives. I have some wishes too.

"I wish I could tell you that this tragedy didn't happen—that it's just a nightmare and we're all going to wake up and everything is all right. But I can't. I wish I could give you a quick fix formula that will lift your pain and answer your questions. But I can't. I wish I could tell you that your pain and grief will vanish quickly and you will go back to normal quickly never to revisit you again. But I cannot. For all of you, as well as all of the body of believers, have been deeply wounded."

And from there we moved into sharing their experiences and discussed grief and trauma, and the steps they could take.

Following this meeting I met with two college-age students who had been severely traumatized by the incident, one by what she saw and the other by being directly involved with those who were killed. Upon hearing shots, the young man went to the van, climbed in amidst the chaos, took off his shirt, and attempted to stop the flow of blood from one of the girls. He stayed to help until the medics and police pried him away from the scene. Eventually he went home, changed clothes, and stayed in his roommate's room for the night. But in the morning he saw his clothes, which he had forgotten to throw away, which re-traumatized him. Both of these young people could hardly talk because of their pain and sobbing. I listened, made a few suggestions about what to do to care for themselves in the next few days, and prayed with them.

I had a half hour remaining until the next large group meeting, but there was no break since one of the pastors said another staff member needed to talk

This event had reactivated a trauma from three years previously. This young woman was the daughter of missionaries in Mexico where they lived and served. She was kidnapped and held hostage for 11 days while the seven kidnappers demanded a ransom. Fortunately, she wasn't mistreated in any way and was returned to her family. But she was taken by gunpoint, and when she heard shots it all came back and she dove under the desk and hid. Later when the police were completing their search, they found her, and when she looked up one had a gun pointed at her, which added to her distress. As we talked I wondered about her anger toward her kidnappers since she said they had taken away her identity by what they did. She didn't think there was any anger, but ten minutes later she realized, "I *am* still angry at them." I encouraged her to write an angry letter to each one and read it aloud.

The next large group session was with over 500 of the churches' small-group leaders. This meeting was structured similar to the first one, but with another emphasis on what *to* do and say and what *not* to do and say to their small-group members. Not only was there insufficient time to do what I wanted to do and the audio-visual resources were inadequate, but just when I began the fire alarm went off and you could see a wide variety of startle responses, hypervigilance, and even one individual went into a full panic attack and hyperventilated.

To help their group leaders the church purchased 400 copies of *Helping Those Who Hurt*. In each group meeting we distributed ten pages of material on grief, crisis, trauma, how to respond, and what to expect, etc. (The church made this available to the entire congregation on Sunday, which was a wise decision.) The pastor and staff are clearly facing not only this trauma but the aftermath created by previous problems. God does redeem tragedy, and He is there in the midst of the deepest difficulty.

Immediately following this meeting we went to the sanctuary for a worship service. An email had been sent to the congregation to gather for worship and prayer and to hear the Word and recognize all those who had helped. And they did come, six to seven thousand of them. It was a rich time of worship and prayer. The lieutenant governor, state attorney general, and the mayor all spoke. The pastor's message was balanced and focused on "Fear not." His words, as quoted in one of the newspapers, were:

> The senior pastor told the members, who altogether number about 10,000, that they would pray for courage.
>
> And they would forgive the killer.
>
> The church family, he said, would extend compassion to the family of the shooter, who ultimately killed himself after taking four other lives.
>
> He said, "We will not be governed by fear. We are people of faith. We are people of hope. Heaven is not rattled by what happened. There is a family in Denver also burying a son," the pastor said. "No matter what happens, the loss of a child is the loss of a child."
>
> He said the congregation would let go of any offense, any hurt.
>
> They would pray for healing for the injured, two in Arvada and three in Colorado Springs. He concluded with, "Lord, give us memories that are from heaven and not from hell."

The congregation was encouraged to walk through the building, the site of the shootings, and the parking lot, and pray over every area and reclaim it for the Lord and His work. As one man said, "I can just remember the few minutes of terror or I can choose to remember the years of blessing."

The worship and singing were amazing, and this service was a positive step in beginning to face the event, the pain, and to move on. The pastor encouraged all those who were directly involved and/ or traumatized in some way to meet with our team for debriefing, but instead of a small group we ended up in a large chapel with about 125 people of all ages, including children. We could see the pain and trauma on their faces. Many had faced the thought they were going to die.

For 45 minutes we led them through a debriefing and provided them with an eight-page handout.

After I talked about the importance of telling their story, either verbally or in writing, a young woman asked if she could share her experience. Several years ago she was at the Columbine incident. When the shooting started, she attempted to hide but was shot two or three times and spent a number of days in the hospital. She stressed the importance of telling the story of what happened for healing to occur. It was amazing how God brought the right people at the right time to aid in the process of healing.

Following the meeting we talked with individuals. At about 9:30 p.m. I realized I was emotionally and spiritually empty and had nothing more to give on this day so I left.

The next morning we met with the other injured family. The mother had been shot in the shoulder while others had been hit by shrapnel and glass. The family with mother, father, their 15- and 20-year-old daughters and a college-age friend had driven around the church and saw the gunman in front of them and thought he had a paintball gun. As they drove slowly toward him, he turned and shot through the windshield. Then they realized this was real. Everyone thought in the next few seconds they were going to die.

There were five of us meeting with the five of them in their living room for close to two hours talking through the incident. Each told their story and interacted with everyone. There were tears, expressions of fear and fright upon faces, and a manifestation of dependence on the Lord, evidence of a strong prayer life and hope for the future. The atmosphere varied from the teary, emotional expression to everyone laughing, which is what happens so much in debriefings.

When there's an opportunity for humor we use it. The pastor in our group opened his Bible to share from Psalm 37 only to discover his dog had chewed out several pages. I don't think he expected me to say, "Well, dog gone." The shock on his face and the collapse into fits of laughter was worth it and served as a needed release.

We talked with them about future triggers of their trauma such as sounds, smells, seeing someone resembling the gunman, images and scenarios in films and TV, and what to avoid and how to handle such.

In the midst of a life-threatening and life-changing experience, their confidence and dependence upon the Lord was a model for all of us. It was a privilege to have been with them. God will use this experience in their lives to minister to others, and they are willing for Him to lead them in this.

During our discussion the teenage girl, whose mother was shot in the shoulder during the event, said, "I made a list of blessings about this experience. May I share this with you?" With her permission, here is what this young girl with the spiked hair and a handwritten sentence on the back of her shirt stating, "Jesus saved my life," said:

> These are true, bona-fide miracles by the hand of God:
>
> - The second shot, through Dad's headrest, should have hit and killed him. In normal driving position, it would have, but he was leaning only a tad forward to get a better look at the guy.
> - Third shot: I have no idea how this did not hit my mom or sisters.
> - Fourth shot: the bullet was fired at *point blank* at our car. It hit Mom in the shoulder, coming in and out cleanly. Missed my dad. My coat, which was on my knees, got hit as I've discovered, and had it not been there, I probably would have had a more serious knee injury. My head was also near my knees, and is untouched as far as I know.

- My sister, who was the most open of the three of us in the backseat, was untouched.

- My other sister, who was also vulnerable to the point-blank shot and just behind Mom, was untouched.

- When our car stalled/died, I believe God did that so that the shooter would move his focus from us.

- My dad is an amazing protector.

- Mom sustained no muscle damage.

- Our car started again.

- Out of five of us in the car, one was wounded and a bullet hit the top of the umbrella. Considering the odds, it's rather ridiculous.

- God got our attention, He sent His angels to guard us and protect us, and they did.

- We survived a hateful attack thanks to my Father on High, the Lord my God who was and is and is to come. He has delivered me from the enemy.

We met with the pastors later that morning. I heard many talk about the gunman and express deep concern for his parents and other family members as well as stating their forgiveness to him.

We planned what to do over the next few weeks and months. How refreshing it was to see a church so willing to take the steps needed for healing and moving on.

I was driven to the airport by a pastor and his wife, and the entire time was spent hearing their story of terror and helping them. The other two members of the team stayed on and spent their time conducting individual and group debriefings.

This deployment was an intense experience. It was an opportunity to minister and to be ministered to, to learn and grow and be blessed. Scripture describes it best:

> Praise be to the God and Father of our Lord Jesus Christ,
> the Father of compassion and the God of all comfort,
> who comforts us in all our troubles, so that we can com-
> fort those in any trouble with the comfort we ourselves
> receive from God. For just as we share abundantly in
> the sufferings of Christ, so also our comfort abounds
> through Christ (2 Corinthians 1:3-6).

We ministered out of our experience, and in the future many of those impacted by this tragedy will minister to others.

Some have asked me, "What about your grief?" You see, my wife of 48 years had passed away two months previously after struggling with brain tumors for four years.

Ministering and helping others is part of my healing process. It's important to reinvest in others. Even as I traveled to Colorado, my mind would travel back to images and thoughts of my wife. But I stayed in my work mode and said, "No, not now. Not at this time," for I knew the effect this could have on me. Maybe there would be an occasion to grieve before returning home and per-haps not. This I could control to some extent, while there would be other triggers that I have no control over whatsoever. But I know the grief hasn't left. It's there, lurking under the surface like a giant bass (what else?) just waiting for that opportunity to engage in a feeding frenzy.

There were a few occasions when it broke through and I was close to having a meltdown, but I realized that my focus at that time needed to be on others and I will tend to myself later when I can really unravel. And I will. I know it's coming in the next few days. It needs to. As I drove home from the airport, about a mile from home I began to feel different. It was as though grief was creeping up on me emotionally like when you're lying in bed and you're cold and you slowly and gently pull a blanket up over you.

Occasionally I felt the grief moving about as though it was look-ing for an opening to surge through. Perhaps the more I tend to restrict it, the more energy it gains. As I write this it seems silent as though sleeping, but I know it will awaken. When? Only grief knows for sure.

The next day it made its presence known. Grief will continue to do this for longer than I want and so I hold on to this promise of the Scripture: "I will turn their mourning into joy. I will comfort them and exchange their sorrow for rejoicing" (Jeremiah 31:13 NLT).

CHAPTER 4

Bouncing Back

All eyes were glued to the young man who stood poised just two inches from the edge of the platform over 200 feet in the air. From his perspective the distance probably seemed as deep as the abyss of the Grand Canyon. The people on the ground looked on with quiet fascination, waiting, just waiting. He lifted one foot a few inches in the air, hesitated, and put it back. Then he took a deep breath, blinked his eyes, and stepped out into space. Down and down he fell until his tether stretched taut. All of a sudden he seemed to rocket back up toward the platform. The elasticity of the bungee line shot him skyward. It had resilience. It had the ability to bounce back.

One of the toys I remember from my childhood was a paddle with a long rubber band and a small ball attached to it. You hit the little ball with the paddle as hard as you could to make it fly out as far as possible, stretching the rubber band to its limit. Let me tell you, it had resilience! Sometimes the ball came flying back at me like a missile, and all too frequently it missed the paddle and hit me! I quickly learned to respect the power of elasticity.

Over the years I've discovered that some people have the capability of bouncing back—they have *resilience*. But others don't. Perhaps you've wondered as I have what makes the difference. Why is it that some people have the ability to bounce back after adversity while others do not? That is the purpose of this book—to discover the way not only to survive but to grow through life's problems.

Stories of survival all around us. The *Reader's Digest* has carried many of them. One *Reader's Digest* told the story of four fishermen from a Central American country. One day as they were out fishing, something happened to their boat. It just wouldn't work anymore. Soon they were caught in the currents and swept out of sight of land and the shipping lanes. The men were adrift for months before they were discovered still alive. The focus of the article was on how they survived.

A newspaper carried the story of a plane crash in the mountains during the heart of winter. The combination of the snowstorms and the rugged terrain prevented the rescuers from getting to the plane for ten days. Facing the worst, they were amazed to discover 14 people still alive. One of the first questions the rescuers asked was, "How did you survive?"

I've asked this in many of the intense events I've worked: "How are you surviving?" There are those who experience never-ending crises. It's one upset after another. Perhaps that's where you or someone you love is living right now. Your crisis could take the form of a devastating illness that destroys all the dreams you've been working toward for years. Or your finances have been drained, and the numbing ache of exhaustion and despair has crept into the life of your family. Perhaps you have a child who has run away from home or chosen a lifestyle totally in opposition to your values. Or what about the family whose eight-year-old girl was struck by a car as she rode her bicycle around a blind corner? That happened 30 years ago, and she still can't speak or move. Thirty years of waiting, hoping, putting their dreams on hold.

How does one survive when over a period of several years two of your adult sons are tragically killed, another son tells you he is gay, and your husband has lost his memory because of a medical problem? This is not fiction. It happened to a friend of mine.

How do you survive the shooting at Miami, Las Vegas, or Sutherland, Texas?

Another friend of mine who ministered to thousands of young people in a camping ministry over the past 20 years, and who was an outstanding songwriter and singer, in time could barely walk. He developed difficulty cutting the food on his plate. His once-skilled hands could no longer play the guitar. He had multiple sclerosis. It would never get better, but he survived 15 years longer than the doctors gave him.

I enjoy receiving not just cards at Christmas but also the newsy letters that tell of the year's events. One friend's letter told the following experience. During the past year, nine of her friends at church were diagnosed with cancer and two subsequently died. She and her husband were involved in a head-on collision with another car. Her husband had kidney stone surgery with complications. His father died later that year. Two friends were sentenced to life in prison, one for poisoning his wife and the other for sexually molesting his granddaughter. Her brother-in-law left his wife and child for cocaine. Her own brother was suicidal and finally entered a program. She was having lunch on an ocean pier with a student from Japan when an elderly man in a wheelchair wheeled himself to the end of the pier near them, lifted himself over the rail, and plunged into the ocean in an attempt to kill himself.

You're probably thinking, *That's unbelievable*, or *That's too much for one person to handle*, or *What an overload!* And that's what is was, an overload—an unexpected overload. But she survived.

Your crisis probably doesn't make the news. Many of them don't. But it's just as major to you and hurts just as much. There are so many life-crushing events like the loss of a child, the loss of a spouse through divorce or death, abuse, a lawsuit, mental illness in your family, being robbed or victimized in other ways. You know what I'm talking about; you can't help but know. The upsets of life are all around us. And now we struggle with terrorism.

Why is it that some people survive the cries and difficulties of life, yet others don't? Why do some overcome the storms of life while others are overwhelmed by them?

Perhaps it's because we think of storms as exceptions to the rule of calm weather. Maybe our perspective is wrong. I propose that times of calm are more likely the exceptions.

A number of years ago I went fishing on a lake in Minnesota with several relatives. It was a beautiful day. As the afternoon wore on, it became very calm and still. Suddenly my cousin said, "Let's head for shore…quick!" I couldn't believe what I was hearing. The weather was great and the fish were beginning to bite. But my cousin said, "Just wait." By the time we made the shoreline, ten minutes later, we were fighting 30- to 40-mile-an-hour winds. They seemed to come out of nowhere. For hours we huddled in our tents just waiting for them to be torn from their pegs.

Where did the storm come from? I wondered. One moment the sky was clear, the next we were being buffeted about by strong winds and a torrential downpour.

Storms are like that. They often appear out of nowhere at the "wrong" time and are totally inconvenient. They disrupt our plans, and some leave devastation in their path. Life is never the same after some storms have swept through our lives.

There are other storms that do give us some warning. They appear gradually, and forecasters are able to give us some indication in advance. You can prepare for these to some degree if the predictions are consistent, but often they aren't, and once again we find ourselves unprepared.

Storms come as all kinds, sizes, shapes, and intensities. There are rainstorms, snowstorms, and windstorms. Nahum the prophet said, "[The Lord's] way is in the whirlwind and the storm" (1:3).

I've been in some storms where the sky was split open by flashing brilliant fingers of lightning followed by ear-deafening thunder. I've stood on the shoreline of Jackson Lake in the Grand Teton National

Park and heard the thunder begin to roll through the Teton range 20 miles to the left of me and continue in front of me on up into Yellowstone National Park. It was a breathtaking, awesome experience.

When we experience a crisis, it seems as though everything is "on the line." How would you define this experience? *Webster's* defines *crisis* as a "crucial time" and "a turning point in the course of anything." This term is often used to describe a person's internal response to some external hazard. When you or I experience an event like this, at first we are thrown off guard and we temporarily lose our ability to cope. Do you know what I'm talking about? Very possibly you do if you've lived any length of time.

You will be able to handle this event better if you understand what it is and the potential that lies within it for your benefit. Far too often we think of crises as the unusual, mostly negative events we should avoid, when they are actually the stuff of which life is made. Why do I say that? Because crises have the potential for developing Christian character in us. "We also glory in our sufferings, because we know that suffering produces perseverance; perseverance, character; and character, hope. And hope does not put us to shame, because God's love has been poured out into our hearts through the Holy Spirit, who has been given to us" (Romans 5:3-5).

Sometimes it's difficult to see any potential, any good, any benefit, or even any way to recover from a crisis. You can look at the front page of the newspaper or watch the first 15 minutes of a newscast to see that crises come in all shapes and sizes.

A businessman who lost his business and had to declare bankruptcy had no vision for his future. He wondered if life would ever be stable again. Not only did he repeatedly ask why, he wondered where God was when he needed Him the most. His crisis challenged his beliefs and faith in God. *How could such a loss have any purpose?* he thought. He felt at loose ends, wondering what his first step would be to move forward. The crushing experience immobilized him.

I can think of a more public example. Perhaps you remember a significant day in sports. One of the best hitters for the Montreal Expos was at the plate facing a hard-throwing pitcher for the San Francisco Giants. The pitcher looked at the runner at first base and then threw as hard as he could. Little did he know it would be the last pitch he would ever throw in any kind of game. A sharp crack was heard all over the stadium as the bone in Dave Dravecky's arm snapped in two. Those watching saw him grasp his arm; later he said that he'd felt it was going to fly toward home plate. They also heard his scream as he fell to the ground.

It wasn't just that his arm was broken. The doctors found that the cancer he thought was in remission had reappeared. His arm had to be amputated at the shoulder to ensure the cancer wouldn't spread to the rest of his body.[1]

Can you imagine the questions and thoughts that would run through your mind if you had just gone through this experience? You're losing part of your body. You're losing the skill you've worked for years to perfect. You're probably asking yourself, *What about my identity? What if the cancer spreads? What are my odds of surviving? How will I make a living now?* Numbness, fear, and dread soon become your companions.

I think of a friend of mine who was driving home from work when he came upon an accident. A car had hit a motorcycle. My friend stopped and went over to the car to see if the occupants were all right. They were. He then walked toward the downed motorcycle and felt a subtle sense of recognition within. As he stepped over the green motorcycle and lifted the visor of the rider's helmet, he recognized the face of his 19-year-old son, who was dead. His entire family entered into a crisis.

When you lose a loved one, there's a large aching hole in your life. Your sense of disbelief coupled with numbness soon evolves to the pain of realizing that the person is dead…gone. My friend felt as though part of him had been cut away when the full reality of his son's death hit him. He thought, *My son will never come through that door again with a smile on his face.* Any future with his son had been destroyed.

With most unexpected events comes another unwelcome guest—the death of a dream. Perhaps one of the best expressions of what we experience when this happens comes from Langston Hughes in his poem "Dreams":

> If dreams die
>
> Life is a broken-winged bird
>
> That cannot fly…
>
> When dreams go
>
> Life is a barren field
>
> Frozen with snow.[2]

I'm sure Sue felt all the emotion inherent in this poem when something happened to devastate her life. Sue was a woman who had a threefold dream: being a wife, a mother, and a missionary. She achieved all three. It seemed as though all her dreams were coming true. She had a husband, two girls, and was serving on a foreign mission field. One day she discovered her husband had been involved in an affair. Now she lives in the States, works as a nurse, and is rearing her girls alone. She tells about the death of her dream:

> There were actually two dreams that died when my husband walked out. One of them was the death of a marriage. I had this vision that I was going to be married for the rest of my life. Now that vision was gone. For a long time I had a mental picture that I was standing at a grave, trying to bury my marriage. The hole was dug, but boards were across the grave so they couldn't put the casket down into the ground. The casket was open and they couldn't continue the burial because I refused to throw

in my flowers. I was holding a dead wedding bouquet, my symbol of my marriage. I hung on to that bouquet for a long time.

I knew I was beginning to heal when the day came in my vision that I wanted to pick up some fresh pink carnations for myself and throw the dead bouquet into the casket. That's when I knew I was beginning to let go of my grief.[3]

We need to grieve over destroyed dreams. But there's something else that can happen to a dream. When it doesn't die but it does get damaged, the dream is altered. Then you have to begin building your dream anew.

I dreamed that my daughter would attend college. After all, I had almost nine years of college and graduate school behind me! And there was another reason I had such high expectations for Sheryl. Our son, Matthew, was profoundly retarded and would never be more than an infant mentally. This added to my desire that Sheryl go to college. Plus, I taught at a Christian university at the time and her tuition would be free.

After one year of college Sheryl said it wasn't for her. After half a semester at fashion design school she dropped out and said she was going to cosmetology school to become a manicurist. Our initial dream was damaged, and we wondered where this new dram would lead. Little did we know what would happen!

Sheryl became one of the leading nail technicians and nail artists in the nation! She won most of the national and international nail competitions. She owned her salon, published her own nail-art book, and was asked to teach and judge events internationally. She reached *her* dreams. Our dreams needed to be altered to line up with hers. There are times when we all need to accept altered dreams in order to move ahead.

Throughout your city or town right now, many people are experiencing their own world-collapsing events. We now live with the fear of terrorist attacks in our community. I've seen the results firsthand and ministered to the survivors.

Most of us experience individual upsets. Consider the following;

- A young man's heart, which had become a receptacle of love for a certain young lady, is now filled with pain he never could have imagined because she said no to his marriage proposal.
- A family has had no income for months. The unemployment checks have run out, and there are no prospects at all for a job.
- A young athlete who has spent 15 years working toward his dream of playing professional ball hears the surgeon say, "Your knee injury is beyond repair."
- A young mother who has gone to check on her three-month-old baby finds that he's a victim of SIDS (Sudden Infant Death Syndrome).
- The 40-year-old man who has just walked out of his doctor's office in a dazed fog is still trying to make sense of the deadly prognosis he's just heard.

The crisis you and I experience can be the result of one event or several. It may be great or overwhelming, such as the death of a child, or it could be a problem that has a special significance just for you that makes it overwhelming. This could be a problem that comes at a time of special vulnerability or when you're unprepared. I'm sure you've had to handle a stopped-up sink. Usually this presents no real difficulty except for the inconvenience. But if the sink stops up when you have the flu and little or no sleep for two nights, you feel overwhelmed. It's the last straw!

If a problem occurs when your coping abilities are not functioning well, or when you don't have the support or help from others that you need, you feel overwhelmed and see the event as overwhelming.

There are three possible outcomes of the unexpected: a change for the better, a change for the worse, or a return to the previous level of functioning.

The word *crisis* is rich with meaning. The Chinese term for crisis (*weiji*) is made up of two symbols: One is for danger and the other for opportunity. The English word is based on the Greek word *krinein*, meaning "to decide." This is a time of decision and judgment as well as a turning point during which there will be a change for the better or worse.

When a doctor talks about crisis, he or she is talking about the moment in the course of a disease when a change for the better or worse occurs. When the counselor talks about a marital crisis, he or she is talking about the turning point when the marriage can go in either direction; it can move toward growth, enrichment, and improvement, or it can move toward dissatisfaction, pain, and in some cases, dissolution. As you think of the crises you've experienced, how did they turn out? A change for the better, for the worse, or back to normal?

You may become stuck—it's so easy to end up being stuck after an unthinkable event. Sometimes we don't know which way to turn. I've been stuck before. We are unable to move, whether it's forward, sideways, or even backward. Stuck means there's no movement. I've been stuck in quicksand and mud in a river. No matter what I tried, it didn't work. I've been stuck in my mind, not knowing which way to move. I needed to make a decision, but my brain wasn't working. My ability to concentrate and make a decision was not there.

Have you been there? Immobilized—that's what it's like to be stuck. I've sat with those who wished they could move, but they couldn't. If you are stuck, you may find the suggestions below helpful or at the very least they may give you some encouragement and hope.

Have you ever wondered why people vary in their response to horrendous events? Why is it that some seem to handle the event so well? Why do some suffer much more intensely than others? If you've watched news interviews, you've seen the variation of survivor's responses. Let's consider why this happens. There is no simple answer.

Everyone is different. We are all wired differently and bring different life experiences and abilities to an event.

When an event occurs, if you were able to do something such as helping others or finding some solution, you will be less upset and frustrated than if you couldn't do anything. As I worked in the aftermath of the Las Vegas shooting, I don't know how many I talked to who were struggling with survivor's guilt. Many said, "I should have…" or "If only…" There was guilt over not being shot while others were or saying, "I should have gone back," or "Why didn't I cover their body?"

There are many who do survive and move forward in life.

There are many who do not survive and remain where they are or even deteriorate. What's the difference?

There are a number of factors that determine who survives and grows and who doesn't:

- This first one is crucial. Those who survive plan ahead in order to prepare for a loss or the unexpected. (That is why you will find suggestions in this book on how to prepare in advance.)

- When it's not possible to plan ahead, they look at others who are resourceful people and learn from them.

- They are not habitual complainers. They find ways to get rid of any negative feelings.

- They are aware of what they can do but ask for help from others when needed. Not only that, they are able to give help when others need assistance.

- They have a desire to learn and grow. They don't want to remain where they are in life.

Before reading on, stop and evaluate where you are in each of the traits mentioned on the previous page on a scale of 0-10.

0	1	2	3	4	5	6	7	8	9	10

It may help to share your perceptions about yourself with another person and ask them to evaluate you as well. Doing this will show that you have a desire to learn and grow.

- As they have grown and matured, they can identify role models who have influenced them in a positive way and they are able to give credit to them for this.

- They accept responsibility for what happens in their life rather than blame others. They learn to be overcomers.

- They develop ways to cope and learn to plan ahead to overcome adversity.

- They have a strong sense of values, which can sustain them in times of difficulty.

- They have an attitude of optimism even during difficult times.

- The enjoyment of life is present whether things are good or not.

- When misfortune hits it doesn't cripple them; rather, they learn from it for both themselves as well as for others' benefit as well.

- They learn to be flexible and adaptable as they work on projects and challenges.

- Their purpose in life is to work for improvement in every area of life.

- They engage challenges with a desire to overcome them.[4]

The blows of life hurt us. But one warning may help: Often those who hurt most are silent, but the screamers are better off than their silent counterparts. At least they know they are hurt and are feeling their pain. For various reasons, we don't allow ourselves to experience the pain we feel.

When a person encounters a traumatic experience, he becomes a wounded individual, and as with all wounds, there must be a time of healing. However, scarring is often the result of the trauma. *Psychic trauma*, a term used in professional circles, is defined as "an emotional state of discomfort and stress resulting from memories of an extraordinary, catastrophic experience which shattered the survivor's sense of invulnerability to harm."[5]

Our assumptions about how we think life should operate form a cognitive or mental frame around reality. Inside the frame we place our deepest hopes, expectations, and dreams. We see ourselves having a wonderful, successful, and beautiful life. But tragedy breaks the picture. Like a portrait falling off the wall and smashing onto the floor, suddenly the frame that surrounds the beautiful portrait of reality is shattered in pieces.[6]

What steps or actions have you done in your past that proved helpful in moving forward? Share your story with someone who is a good listener and not judgmental.

It would be helpful to look for advice from a counselor who has experience in this area.

Look for books or even research on the internet that would address your situation. Each day look for something new to learn and begin making a list of what you have learned and how you are different.

Make a list of your abilities and strengths. Share your list with others and ask them to add to your list.

Describe what you will be like a year from now. What will you need to do to achieve this?

What can you do today to help someone else?

CHAPTER 5

The Phases—They're Normal

You open your eyes but you can't see clearly. You blink. Everything is hazy, as though you were in a thick fog. There's a sense of unreality in everything around you. You feel as though you've been run over by a two-ton truck. You blink again, but your view of the world is still a bit fuzzy. Are you losing your mind? Were you in an accident? Did someone hit you? Probably none of the above.

Welcome to the world of the unexpected or unthinkable! When you and I enter that state called "crisis time," we feel as though we've grabbed hold of an electrical wire! As you read about the four phases inherent in this situation, keep in mind that the time to transition through each phase will vary for each of us. Don't compare your experience with the approximate time suggested for getting through each phase. You could experience an intense crisis that prolongs a certain stage for months. And if you face another crisis before resolving the first one, the situation is compounded, further delaying each stage.

Why is it important to know about these? By knowing about them you will

- realize that you're not going crazy; you're just going through a normal passage.

- relieve some of the pain and pressure by recalling that, "Oh, yes, this phase will pass and I'll go on to the next one."

- recognize there's a light at the end of the tunnel—there is hope and new life.

- gain control of your life and the outcome sooner by knowing what to expect.

As writer Ann Stearns put it:

> Recovery from loss is like having to get off the main highway every so many miles because the first route is under reconstruction. The road signs reroute you through little towns you hadn't expected to visit and over bumpy roads you hadn't wanted to bounce around on. You are basically traveling in the appropriate direction. On the map, however, the course you are following has the look of shark's teeth instead of a straight line. Although you are gradually getting there, you sometimes doubt that you will ever meet up with the finished highway. *There is a finished highway in your future.* You won't know when or where, but it's there. You will discover a greater sense of resilience when you know in advance what you will experience and that you're normal in your response.[1]

The first stage of a crisis is called the *impact phase*. The intensity of a person's response to a crisis varies, but all of us feel the impact. You know immediately that something drastic has happened to you. You're stunned. It's as if someone has hit you over the head with a two-by-four and you're seeing stars.

Often with these events we enter into a fog. It's a fog of disbelief. "No, this isn't happening, not to me—not now—not to us." For some this fog is impenetrable—you can't adjust to the reality in your head.[2] It may be denial, or you may just be stunned.

Except in extremely dire cases, we tend to display a surprisingly creative and willful brand of denial. This denial can take the form of delay, which can be fatal, as it was for some on 9/11. But why do we do it if it is so dangerous?

How long the delay lasts depends in large on how we calculate risk.

We know something is terribly wrong, but we don't know what to do about it. How do we decide? The first thing to understand is that nothing is normal when we are in a crisis. We think and perceive differently. We become superheroes with learning disabilities.

Many—if not most—people tend to shut down entirely in a disaster, quite the opposite of panicking. They go slack and seem to lose all awareness.[3] They don't respond in a healthy survival mode. Listen to this description:

> When it comes to old-fashioned risks like weather, we often overestimate ourselves. Of the fifty-two people who died during Hurricane Floyd in 1999, for example, 70 percent drowned. And most of them drowned in their cars, which became trapped in floodwaters. This is a reoccurring problem in hurricanes. People are overconfident about driving through water, even though they are bombarded with official warnings not to. (This tendency varies, of course, depending on the individual. One study out of the University of Pittsburgh showed that men are much more likely to try to drive through high water than women—and thus more likely to die in the process…)
>
> Even in times of calm, we trend toward arrogance. About 90 percent of drivers think they are safer than the average driver. Most people also think they are less likely than others to get divorced, have heart disease, or get fired. And three out of four baby boomers think they look younger than their peers…

Risk analysists call these emotional judgments...or... "faint whispers of emotion."[4]

Resilience is a precious skill. People who have it tend to also have three underlying advantages: a belief that they can influence life events; a tendency to find meaningful purpose in life's turmoil; and a conviction that they can learn from both positive and negative experiences. These beliefs act as a sort of buffer, cushioning the blow of any given disaster. Dangers seem more manageable to these people, and they perform better as a result.[5]

If you are, for whatever reason, particularly frightened of something that is not on your risk list, then prepare for it, too. The more control you feel you have, the less dread you will feel day to day. And the more control you feel, the better your performance will be, should the worst come to pass.

Disaster experts think about disasters for a living, but they don't feel powerless. They do things to give their brains shortcuts in the unlikely event they need them. They always look for their nearest exit when they board planes, for example. And they read the safety briefing cards that most people think are useless. They do this because each plane model is different, and they know they may become functionally retarded in a plane crash.[6]

For some who see the event unfolding before them, there's a sense of panic and fear. This happens even to those who are observers of an impending event. The "Oh no!" response is normal when you see a major tragedy about to occur and there's nothing you can do to stop it. I've experienced this more than once. It's not a pleasant experience.

Years ago I was driving home in the late afternoon from teaching my classes at the graduate school at Biola University. I turned onto Stage Road, which ran parallel to the Amtrak train tracks, and then made another turn onto a cross street. Because a train was due in less than a minute, the crossing arms had come down to prevent drivers from crossing the tracks.

As I sat waiting in line, several drivers became impatient and began to drive around the crossing arm and across the tracks. Out of the corner of my eye I saw the passenger train hurtling down the track as a VW Beetle began to sneak across. In that split second I knew what was going to happen. And with that knowledge, I let out an anguished cry of "Oh no" and actually yelled at the train!

Then it happened. The train plowed into the small car and dragged the twisted metal hundreds of feet along the track. Turning my car out of the line of stopped traffic, I drove to a pay phone and called for help. As I drove home, my mind and body were in shock. I think I prayed and talked out loud the entire way home.

When I got home I saw my wife, Joyce, and our daughter by the car. Sheryl had her driving permit and was getting into the driver's seat. I pulled up, got out of the car, and said to them, "Sheryl is *not* driving anywhere today," then went into the house. They were shocked at my outburst and followed me inside. They found me in the family room, pacing back and forth. I started to tell them what had happened, expressing my horror through tears. It took years for the crash images to lose their sense of reality.

The next day I learned that the driver was a young Biola student and the daughter of one of the professors. Fortunately, she survived, although it took her months to recover. It took me years not to be hypervigilant when I drove over that crossing twice a day.

Another time I had just walked into my bedroom and heard a helicopter flying overhead. The sound wasn't the normal pitch of an engine, so I rushed outside. I looked up and saw the helicopter twisting and turning as it flew on, apparently out of control. It continued to veer one way and then another as the pilot fought to maintain control. About a mile away the helicopter plunged straight down.

During this time, I was saying, "Oh no! It can't be!" Part of my worry came from its proximity to a friend's home.

Later I learned that tragedy was averted when the craft hit wires that broke its fall. The three occupants escaped with minor injuries. But I still experienced that state of panic.

The impact phase is usually brief, lasting from a few hours to a few days, depending upon the event and person involved. Some impact phases linger on and on because of the intensity of the event and our life experiences.

The more severe the crisis or loss, the greater the impact and the greater the amount of incapacitation and numbness. Tears may be an immediate part of this phase or they may come later on.

The earliest response to the unexpected is the overall numbing that sets in. An individual's defense system takes over to buy time and help him adjust to the extreme nature of the stressor that seeks to tear apart his emotional well-being. The numbing has a spillover effect, creating a diminished interest in the usual activities of life. The person may feel detached or estranged from those he loves most. Psychologists talk about the "flat affect" that characterizes this symptom. The facial posture is flat and unresponsive. There is no twinkle in the eye, and it is as if the eyes have become hollow or vacant.[7]

During this phase, one of the questions you must answer is, "Should I stay and face the problem or withdraw and run from it?" This is called the fight-or-flight pattern. With fires, shootings, or hurricanes, we usually want to run.

A number of years back, an advertisement espoused the words, "I'd rather fight than switch." Not everyone feels that way. If your tendency in the past has been to face problems, you will probably face this head-on. But if your tendency has been to avoid or withdraw from problems, you'll probably do the same with this event. If the event is especially severe, you may feel like running anyway because you're not as able to cope during this phase.

Most of the time running is not the solution. It merely prolongs the situation. And since there are several more phases of a crisis yet to come before balance is restored, why linger in this phase? Why prolong the pain? Facing it and fighting to regain control is usually the healthier response if that's possible.

Don't expect your thinking to be clear during this time. You'll feel numb and disoriented. You may even feel as though you can't think or feel at all. Someone described it this way: "I feel as though my entire system shut down." You need to watch your driving since at this time you are likely to get in an accident or get a ticket.

Your mind is impacted, as is your body. You will need to lower your expectations of yourself. Some may sleep more, but you may struggle with sleeping well since your brain is still active, especially the right side, the picture and emotional side. Some nightmares are repetitive and intense. If this is true in your case, just before you turn out the light, sit on the side of your bed and handwrite the nightmare until you come to the end of it and then write a new positive end to it. This tends to break the pattern and control of the nightmare.

You will probably replay the event in your mind time and time again purposely as well as in flashbacks or intrusive pictures. For some it's like watching the rerun of a movie while others see still pictures.

Your ability to process information is limited. If a friend or family member attempts to share any factual information with you, it sails right over your head. You may ask, "What did you say?" even though the person has repeated it for the third time. What you experienced affects how you think—clarity and concentration will diminish. You may forget what you were thinking or talking about. Even though you may be organized and functional, this ability may wane as you struggle to follow through. You may feel as though your mind isn't working right. Don't despair when this happens. It's a normal response; most people experience this.

It's best if you don't have to make any important decisions at this time, but if you do, ask a competent friend to help you.

At the heart of most events is a loss of some kind. Losses threated our security, our sense of stability, our well-being. Self-image may be affected, and you feel out of control. The more sudden the loss, the more out of control you will feel. Although a gradual loss is still painful, you can prepare for it to some degree. But a sudden, unexpected death or other unexpected event may disrupt your ability to activate the emotional resources you need in order to cope with the loss.

One of the most difficult losses to deal with is the *threat* of loss. For some, it is like we're waiting for something to happen. The loss has not yet occurred, but there's a real possibility that it will happen. And we think the worst.

Any kind of loss has a way of changing our lives in a dramatic way and affects the way we think about the future. These changes can actually be positive and eventually enrich our lives. But during the first few months it doesn't feel that way at all. If someone were to tell you at the time of a loss that you can learn and grow through it, you might react with disgust, anger, or disbelief. You aren't ready to handle thoughts like that. You can only hear such comments when life is more stable.

During this phase your thought life focuses on the experience in an effort to find what you have lost. It's normal to search for something that meant a great deal to you. You're trying to hold on to your emotional attachments for a bit longer. You're trying to recapture the lost dream, the loved one, or even your health. The more your loss meant to you, the more you will search!

This searching behavior often takes the form of reminiscing. How much you reminisce is in proportion to the value of what you lost. It's common (and healthy) for a person who loses a loved one in death to pour over photographs and other items that remind him or her of the person who died.

There are several things you can do to work through this phase. In fact, these action steps will help you deal with your loss and grief in a healthy way. What do you need to do most during this phase?

1. Accept what has happened. But not only that, accept your feelings and reminisce.

Remember, too, that your emotions have been altered. At first you may experience numbness. You may feel as though you're emotionally depleted or life is now in constant slow motion. You feel sluggish. Anger is usually present, if not at first, then later on. You may range from sadness to depression.

It's normal to express as many feelings as you can. It may be difficult at first to experience your feelings because of the numbness, but when the numbness wears off, your feelings can be intense. This intensity may increase and carry into the next phase. You may even find yourself emotionally exhausted.

2. You need a safe environment in which to grieve and adjust.

Avoid those people who try to make you stifle your feelings. Feelings should not be buried or denied at this point. Rejected feelings delay the resolution of the problem. When feelings are buried, they do not go away; they are simply frozen. Eventually they'll be resurrected.

Do you know what happens to water when it freezes? The ice actually expands. Water frozen in pipes has the power to burst those steel pipes wide open. When we lock up a summer mountain cabin for the winter, it's important to drain all of the water from the pipes if we want them to function properly the next spring. The analogy holds when we speak of frozen emotions. They can expand and take on a power out of proportion to their original nature, so it's important during this time to keep the channels open so that feelings can flow when they need to.

Avoid those who are full of advice and say things like, "I told you so" or "Spiritual Christians get over their hurt sooner than others." Find those who are empathetic and know how to minister to you during a crisis. The people who can help you most have these qualities:

- They don't shock easily but accept your feelings.
- They're not embarrassed by your tears. They encourage them.
- They don't give unwanted advice.
- They're warm and affectionate with you, according to your needs.
- They help you recall your strengths when you've forgotten you have strengths.
- They trust you'll be able to come through this difficult time.
- They treat you like an adult who can make your own decisions.
- They may become angry with you, but they don't attack your character.
- They understand that grief is normal, and they understand the stages of grief.
- They don't spiritualize everything.
- They're sensitive to where you are spiritually and do not try to force feed you theology and Scripture.[8]

Make a list of those who fit these characteristics.

_____

_____

_____

_____

_____

_____

Cultivate friendships with those people *before* your life-changing event occurs. But remember, we draw this kind of people to us as we demonstrate *we're* that kind of people too.

People talk to release their feelings since that's what they know best. Others may empty themselves of their emotions in physical ways. Don't compare yourself with others and say one way of release is the only way or the best way. Some talk about their hurt and grief; others act it out. You may have a friend who spends time working in his yard or doing some other kind of activity but doesn't talk about his loss. Everyone may process their grief in their own way. How do you usually deal with your grief?

For some, rigorous physical activity can bring about healing. I've heard many stories of processing grief, but this one stuck with me. It was from a man who lost his father in a tragic fire. He lived near his father on an adjacent farm. One night the home in which he was born and raised burned to the ground with his father inside. His response to this tragedy startled other family members. He remained silent while they all wept and talked about the loss, then he borrowed a bulldozer and proceeded to bulldoze the ashes and charred remains of the house.

Rain had stopped the fire, and this was his expression of burying his father. He worked for hours, not even stopping for meals or rest. When darkness came, he continued to work, ignoring the requests of family members to stop for the night. Instead, he continued to bulldoze the remains of the house back and forth, again and again.

This man and his father were farmers, and for most of their lives they had worked together in the fields. They didn't verbalize much together or share their feelings. But theirs was a close nonverbal relationship.

You and I may grieve with tears. He grieved with his borrowed bulldozer. This was his personal expression of words and tears. He cried by working the land over and over again until nothing was visible. He gave his father and the home a proper burial in his own way. The land, which in a sense was his father's cemetery, was now ready to be farmed, and it would be—by the son.

If you were to ask him why he had done this, he couldn't give you an answer. We don't always have an answer. He didn't know why he had acted out his grief in this way, but he had done something with his grief, and it was probably the best thing he could have done. We don't always have to know why.

The more immobilized you are by your grief, the more dependent and helpless you feel. Doing something—anything—whether it makes sense to anyone else or not—is a healthy step. It assists you as a beginning step to feeling you have some control again.

3. Be aware that guilt may become your unwelcome companion.

Sometimes guilt causes us to respond in a variety of ways we wouldn't normally respond, from rationalizing and blaming to self-punishment or attempts at atonement. Guilt may try to consume you.

Isn't it interesting how we tend to hook into guilt and end up pointing our finger back at ourselves? Self-blame is usually unrealistic and harsher than the blame we place on others. Our imagination takes the event and magnifies our sense of responsibility. We tell ourselves things like, "If only…" or "I should have…" Some feel guilty for living. Listen to some of the statements common to self-blame:

- "If only I hadn't allowed him to buy that motorcycle. If only I'd instead he wear his helmet, he wouldn't be paralyzed now. I should have been home that night. If I'd been there, the accident wouldn't have happened."

- "I kick myself all over for not telling Mom I loved her. She's not here now and I can't let her know. That opportunity is gone forever. The accident has destroyed us."

- "If I hadn't spent so much time at work, she wouldn't have left me. I was just trying to provide, but I guess I blew it. I kick myself again and again."

- "I should have noticed his depression. I just didn't believe what he was saying, and now he's dead. By his own hand."

- "Where did we go wrong with that child? I guess we were too young and too ignorant. We blew it and she's in trouble because of us."

Time and time again I heard expressions of survivor's guilt after the Las Vegas tragedy; the "I should…" and "If onlys…" were prevalent.

Let's summarize what happens to you during the impact phase, which may last a few hours or even a few days. During this time you'll want to face the situation and fight, or you'll want to run; you will probably think in a somewhat numb and disoriented fashion; you'll search for whatever it is you have lost, often by reminiscing; you will need people to accept your feelings.

You may fluctuate between being overcautious and taking unnecessary risks. You wonder why you are responding in this way but can't seem to make changes. And you could be on edge or hypervigilant.

Remember, your view of the future or belief about life is altered. One of the worst changes is that your sense of safety has been ripped away. This is one of the things you will need to work on since it can take months and years to rebuild.

After the impact phase you're going to move into the *withdrawal-confusion phase*. This will last for days or even weeks, and you will feel emotionally drained. You're worn out. Remember, the various phases overlap one another, and you may move between different phases. That, too, is normal.

During this phase the tendency to deny your feelings is probably stronger than at any other time. One reason is because your feelings now can become the ugliest and most potent. As one emotion triggers another, you may feel intense anger at whatever has occurred, which in some cases brings on guilt for having such feelings. Then you feel shame. The pain from these varied responses increases your desire to repress them. If some of your feelings shock others, you may want to repress them even more.

Expect your feelings to run wild. This is a normal response. In fact, you'll probably feel a sense of

- bewilderment: "I never felt this way before."
- danger: "I feel so scared. Something terrible is going to happen."
- confusion: "I can't think clearly. My mind doesn't seem to work."
- impasse: "I'm stuck. Nothing I do seems to help."
- desperation: "I've got to do something, but I don't know what to do."
- apathy: "Nothing can help me. What's the use of trying!"
- helplessness: "I can't cope by myself. Please help me."
- urgency: "I need help *now*."
- discomfort: "I feel so miserable and unhappy."

I've heard these time and time again.

During the withdrawal-confusion phase, your thinking patterns will reflect a certain amount of uncertainty and ambiguity. You just aren't sure what to think or do.

You'll alternate between bargaining and detachment. Bargaining involves wishful thinking: "If only this hadn't happened"; "If only I could capture what I had"; "Perhaps there's some way to bring back what I had"; "God, if only…"

This type of thinking then moves to the detachment level. You need to detach yourself from whatever it was you lost, whether it is a job, a friend, or a house. A widower cannot stay married to a deceased wife. A student can no longer be a student in the school from which he was expelled. A worker cannot fulfill a job he or she has lost. You distance yourself by saying, "It wasn't that important"; "I can do better now that he or she isn't in my life anymore"; "I wanted a new job anyway." You do this to ease the pain of your loss. One way to accomplish this is to write a good-bye letter to what or whomever you've lost.

You may find yourself vacillating between performing some tasks that need to be done and then reflecting and reminiscing on how things used to be. You may feel anger at having to give up what you lost, whether it is a person, an object, or an identity. We try to protect ourselves from the emptiness that loss brings. In our attempt to restore what is gone, we tend to distort and glorify the past. We do this to help us face the future. As we reach out to others and even to new people, we do it in an attempt to fill the void in our lives.

During this time you need the assistance of caring friends and relatives to help you organize your life. You could need help in planning your day, arranging appointments, keeping the house or job in order, and so on. Don't be hard on yourself for this apparent weakness in your life. It's a normal transition through your upset, and it's not a defect. For example, the period of grief over the loss of a house is not the time to be looking for another partner. It's a time to adjust to the loss.

There is one additional source of pain you'll need to contend with: others who make statements that hurt rather than console, hinder rather than comfort, and prolong your pain rather than relieve it. These people are secondary wounders. They will give you unwanted and bad advice as well as improperly applied scripture.

You won't be the first to experience this. Remember Job? Job had four well-meaning but insufferable friends who came over to cheer him up and try to explain his suffering. They said that anybody with enough sense to come in out of the rain should know that God was just. They said that anybody old enough to spell his own name knew that since God was just, He made bad things happen to bad people and good things happen to good people. They said that such being the case, you didn't need a Harvard diploma to figure out that since bad things had happened to Job, then *ipso facto* he must have done something bad himself. But Job hadn't, and he said so, and that's not all he said either.

In Job 13:2, Job calls these men "miserable comforters." Verses 4-5 go on to record Job saying, "Worthless physicians are you all. Oh that you would keep silent, and it would be your wisdom" (ESV). These "friends" were a bunch of theological quacks, in other words, and the smartest thing they could have done was shut up. But they were too busy explaining things to listen.[9]

Moralizing is not the same as spiritual wisdom. Those who don't know what to say violate what the book of Proverbs instructs us to do and offer clichés and untruths instead. Look at the truth of Proverbs:

> Don't talk so much. You keep putting your foot in your mouth. Be sensitive and turn off the flow! (Proverbs 10:19 TLB).

> Some people like to make cutting remarks, but the words of the wise soothe and heal (Proverbs 12:18 TLB).

> The tongue of the wise speaks knowledge that is pleasing and acceptable, but the mouth of the [babbling] fool spouts folly (Proverbs 15:2 AMP).

> Death and life are in the power of the tongue, and those
> who love it and indulge it will eat its fruit and bear the
> consequences of their words (Proverbs 18:21 AMP).

Expect to hear statements you'd rather not hear. It's difficult to respond to these people the way we would like to because of our traumatized state. Perhaps they would learn not to make such harmful statements if someone spoke up and said, "That's not true and it's not helpful. If you want to be helpful I would appreciate it if you would…" Sometimes we excuse what these people say as well-meaning, which is questionable. Sometimes they're just reflecting their own anxiety, fear, or lack of having dealt with issues in their own lives. Remember, this is not advice coming from experts.

Those who share with you in this manner need to be avoided or educated! During this phase, when the numbness has worn off, you will begin to feel the pain of hearing comments such as these.

To summarize, in the withdrawal-confusion phase (which will last for days, sometimes for weeks), your response will be emotional. You may feel anger, fear, guilt, even rage. Your thinking processes will feel muddled. You will vacillate from bargaining to working on detaching yourself from the lost person or situation.

During this time of puzzled searching for a way out of the difficulty, you need some task-oriented support and help from others. You need others to help you make some plans and accomplish small tasks so that you can feel functional. Don't hesitate to let people know that you want to do something or that you need to feel useful.

The third phase, called the *adjustment phase*, will take weeks to work through. If a new upset occurs, you'll experience a setback. If you have multiple setbacks or losses, work on one at a time or you'll be overwhelmed. But the emotional responses you experience during this time are focused toward hope. Yes, you may feel some depression that comes and goes, but you've started to form positive attitudes again. You may begin to talk about the future with hope and look forward to enjoying a new job, moving to a new location, rebuilding a fire-destroyed home, considering remarriage. You've just about completed your detachment from what you've lost. You are looking around for something new to which you can develop an attachment.

Your future dreams or action steps start to take on special significance to you. You've been in and through the depths of the valley, and you're now climbing up the side of the mountain. Be prepared for the opinions and advice of others, and sift through what you hear.

Others may not see the value of what you are doing now. They could question your decisions and actions if what you're doing doesn't jive with what they think you need to do. Some people may feel that you're making a drastic mistake as you take a new step. Are these people experts?

Don't make any important decisions during your down times; wait until you feel hope. And don't despair because your feelings fluctuate. Your insight is returning and your objectivity can help you process information and new suggestions.

Scripture can assist you in making decisions during this phase. You're more receptive now and capable of dealing with spiritual insights. Prior to this point, Scripture and prayer resources were there to support and sustain you. Now is the time to seek answers and direction through the teaching and reading of the Word.

The final phase (which can last the longest) is the *reconstruction-reconciliation phase*. A key element here is your spontaneous expressions of hope. Your sense of confidence has returned, and you can make plans again. You're able to consciously decide *not* to engage in self-pity anymore.

Initiative, *progress*, and *reattachment* are key words during this period of time. You've assimilated into your life new places, new activities, new people, new jobs, and new spiritual insights. If your feelings of anger and blame create difficulty during this crisis, now is the time to reconcile with those people you may have offended.

One sign of crisis resolution is the newness of life you feel and the new discoveries you experience. This is an opportunity for you to gain new strengths, new perspectives on life, new appreciation, new values, and a new way to approach the way you live. You will look at life differently. Hopefully you will not take it for granted. I know this firsthand.

Several years ago I experienced some strange physical symptoms. These included vertigo, pressure in the back of the head, and headaches. These symptoms persisted for about seven weeks, during which time the doctors had some theories but nothing concrete. My own concerns and worries about what this might be added to some of the feelings I experienced.

Finally, after going through further examinations, including a CAT scan, the symptoms disappeared. As we pieced together what had occurred, we felt the physical symptoms were brought on by too many strenuous seminars with no recuperation time in between, coupled with a cold and some altitude changes. I was experiencing a burnout.

Physical exhaustion is one of the greatest culprits of mysterious ailments. But this experience, especially at the age of 47, caused me to think, reevaluate, and consider some changes in my life. I learned to pace my work in a more balanced manner. I learned to play more and evaluate what was important and what wasn't. I began to say no. I didn't necessarily like what I went through, but I grew because of it and felt it was a necessary experience.

These kinds of experiences can become the means to exciting growth. I've always been impressed with William Pruitt and his response to a physical problem he conquered. In many ways his crisis was with him for the rest of his life. In his book *Run from the Pale*

Pony, Pruitt uses an analogy to describe what happened in his life. I've used his story many times. In the foreword he writes:

> About thirty years ago, one of my joys as a boy was to ride a white horse named Prince. That proud, spirited stallion carried me where I wanted to go, wherever I bid him to and at the pace which I chose. I don't have to explain to horsemen the feeling of strength, even authority, which comes from controlling such a powerful animal. Nor need I expand upon the excitement I felt when I galloped him at full speed, or about the quiet pride that came when I twisted him through the corkscrew turns of a rodeo exercise. After all, he was mine and I trained him. Those experiences are part of my heritage.
>
> My cherished white horse was gone and seldom remembered about fifteen years later. It was then that I encountered a completely different kind of horse. When I first became aware of the specter, its shape was too dim to discern. I know only that I had never seen anything like it before. Too, I know that I had not sought any such creature, yet something different was with me whenever I went and that shadow would not go away. No matter what I did, though, the specter followed my every move. Furthermore, the harder I tried to lose it, the clearer the creature's form became to me.
>
> My uneasiness changed to anxiety when I realized that this unwanted shadow had a will of its own. The chill of fear came when I understood that it had no intention of leaving me alone. Without further warning, it began to communicate with me openly one day, and in a harsh voice which was almost rigid with animosity, it spat out, "You can no longer go wherever you want to go when you choose at the speed you pick. That's true, because I

will give you weakness instead of strength. Excitement and pride? Never again will you have them like before. I plan only confinement and disability for you. And I will be your constant companion. My name is Chronic Illness."

At the time I heard it speak, I shrank back from actually seeing it face to face. It spoke harshly of miseries which were inverse to joys with my white horse named Health and the bitter irony was reflected in the form of a malicious creature. Chronic Illness took the shape of a stunted, misshapen pony. Its shaggy coat was pale in color, streaked with ages-old accumulation of dark despair. But, unquestionably, the most frightening feature of the animal was its overwhelming glare, its glare-eyed stare which held me helpless. The pony's wild eyes starred restlessly from side to side, yet strangely were unbinding. This book is written first for all those people how have met the pale pony face to face.[10]

The "pale pony" might come in many possible forms—serious physical or mental illness, accident, war, or an injury. Whatever shape the pony takes, the results can be quite similar. William Pruitt's pale pony was multiple sclerosis. He sensed that the disease was increasingly affecting his life, but his story is the story of hope. He realized that he had a number of years before he would be completely disabled, and realizing that he wouldn't be able to carry on the type of work he was in, he went back to college in a wheelchair. He earned a PhD in economics and began to teach on a college level.

Pruitt's book is not about giving up; rather, it is about fighting back and winning. It is a very honest book, telling of the pain and the hurt and the turmoil. But its emphasis is on faith and hope.

You may not be able to do what you used to do; your life might not return to the way it was. But you can look for alternatives. You can discover different ways of responding. You can learn to say, "I will be able to *discover* plan B. There *is* a different way to my life!"

Remember, too, this is an opportunity! It is a time for change and growth. There is one factor—attitude—that causes a major crisis to become a growth-producing experience instead of a restrictive, crippling, eternal tragedy. Our world is unstable; it rocks our boat. We are unstable; we rock our boat. But if our attitude has been built upon the teachings of the Word of God, that is our hope in the midst of an upset world! Isaiah 33:6 says, "And He will be the stability of your times" (NASB).

Our stability comes from allowing Jesus Christ to be our rock at all times.

CHAPTER 6

Your Brain: Treat It Well

The game is just about ready to begin. There are 22 beefed-up men glaring at one another. Each one is a physical specimen. Their muscles seem to ripple underneath their stretched uniforms. Each player wears thick pads to protect his muscles. But the most important item of clothing is not their shirt or pants—it's the helmet. Thousands of dollars have gone into research to create the most protective headgear available. But what are they trying to protect? It's their brain. For many years from preadolescence through adulthood, players have experienced brutal blows to their head. This can result in symptoms such as:

- Headache or a feeling of pressure in the head
- Temporary loss of consciousness
- Confusion or feeling as if in a fog
- Amnesia
- Dizziness or "seeing stars"
- Ringing in the ears
- Nausea
- Vomiting

- Slurred speech
- Delayed response to questions
- Appearing dazed

These symptoms indicate a concussion. Many football players experience multiple concussions over the years, which can lead to brain damage that can affect other portions of the body. There is chaos in the brain. Effects are usually temporary but can linger, including headaches and problems with concentration, memory, balance, and coordination. They're usually caused by a blow to the head, but violently shaking the head and upper body can also cause them. It's possible to have a concussion and not realize it.

How else could we describe this portion of your body?

> Imagine a giant Christmas light—as large as a shopping mall—made of an estimated 85 billion light bulbs, all connected by crisscrossing wires. Each wire touches thousands of others, creating 100 trillion touch points. Now shrink this light to the size and shape of a cantaloupe. You are beginning to design nature's finest work of art—your brain.[1]

Your brain has the consistency of gelatin. It's cushioned from everyday jolts and bumps by cerebrospinal fluid inside your skull. A violent blow to your head and neck or upper body can cause your brain to slide back and forth forcefully against the walls of your skull.

But football isn't the only cause for concussion in our brain. Experiencing the unexpected or the unthinkable can lead to an emotional and cognitive concussion. Chaos is created in our brain and leads to what we now know as PTSD—post-traumatic stress disorder or trauma. Sometimes it's easier to recover from the physical impact creating a concussion than from the damage created by a traumatic event.

Our brains have two distinct parts. The left side of our brain speaks one language, and the right side speaks another. This right side is the emotional side. It's intuitive, visual, and spatial. This side carries the music of experience. It stores the memories of the senses, such as sounds, touch, and smell. It's full of pictures that run like a silent movie.

Our left side of the brain is the chatterbox. It controls all the talking. It remembers facts, statistics, and the vocabulary of events. It's full of words and narration. It's the seat of logic. But for this side to describe, tell a story, or share an autobiographical narration, it needs to reach over to the right side and draw on the emotional memories stored there. That's what *should* happen. But here's the problem for those who are traumatized. The left and right sides don't get together that well. The growth of the connection between the two sides has been hampered by that unexpected event.[2]

Traumatized people have alterations in their brains. Your memory could be affected, which often creates lapses and deficits in verbal ability and short-term memory. Imaging scans clearly show that past trauma activates the right hemispheres of the brain and deactivates the left.[3] Trauma is intrusive and invasive. It interrupts and derails us. It can constrict and limit our lives significantly. Sometimes we alternate between the two sides of the brain. We find ourselves caught between amnesia and reliving the trauma; between floods of intense feeling and arid states of no feelings whatsoever; between irritable impulsive action and complete inhibition of action.[4]

Let's think about your brain. It is actually the culprit for much of our discomfort and our growth.

The brain has a tremendous tendency to habituate, meaning to do the same thing over and over—which is great when you don't want to have to think about how you brush your teeth, but not so good when you need to think creatively about how to cope with a situation you've never been in before. That's why we so often tend to keep doing what we've already done, whether we get good results or not, and are slow to give up some behaviors. Remember this word...*habituate.*

To add to the problem, part of habituation is the brain's tendency to look for patterns, to match current experience with the past—*Oh, this is just like that thing that happened before.*

There's an adaptive reason for this habituation. The brain is always on and consumes a disproportionate part of the body's energy.

When the environment is stable, this autopilot serves us well. But during change, we have to fight against our brain's tendency to look at the situation and see the same old thing when it's actually encountering something new.[5] Especially if it's something bad or painful.

"The brain is hard-wired to scan for the bad, and when it inevitably finds negative things, they get stored immediately and made available for rapid recall."[6]

The brain is actually hardwired to act in ways that protect us when we are in dangerous situations. The problem is that the alarm section of our brain is always scanning for danger even when it isn't there. It gives us inaccurate information. It sounds alarms even when it doesn't have to.

In contrast, positive experiences are usually registered through standard memory systems. They actually need to be held in conscious awareness for 10 to 20 seconds for them to really sink in. In sum, your brain is like Velcro for negative experiences and Teflon for positive ones...this built-in bias puts a negative spin on the world and intensifies our stress and reactivity. Basically, the alarm section reacts. And when it does, it's in the driver's seat and you're going along for the ride. Like it or not, you're a passenger. The alarm section has an override button on the other sections of your brain. And it's true that you can't think when it's in control.

So what can you do with these tendencies of the brain that override us? We can work on accessing another portion of our brain, the executive function. How? Consider the following plan.[7]

Have you ever been hijacked? Your answer is probably, "No, of course not." Many of you reading this book probably saw the movie *Captain Phillips* with Tom Hanks, in which his large ship was taken over or hijacked by Somalian pirates. This is the kind of scenario that comes to mind when hijacking is mentioned. But let's return to the question, "Have you ever been hijacked?" A more accurate answer is probably, "Yes, I have." Many of us have, but we didn't realize it. Whenever we experience the unexpected, the possibility is there. The alarm section is responsible for this.

There is a portion of your brain that's always on the alert for the worst. It's like a radar constantly searching. If there is the slightest indication of a problem or pain or the unthinkable, it turns on its switch and wants to get into the action. Sometimes this portion of your brain is referred to as the alarm section or smoke detector. Its real name is the amygdala, but who wants to try to remember that?

Let's look at your brain again. We've talked about the alarm portion. Actually, this portion is activated by both positive and negative experiences, but it registers negative more than positive. This section has been called the panic button of the brain. It would be easier if we had a switch that we could throw like a lever on the train tracks to send the brain in a totally different direction. There is also the front part of your brain, which is the *prefrontal cortex* or the executive part. It makes assessments. It helps you observe what is happening and make conscious choices. It could be called the supervisor.

The *frontal lobes* are one of the most important parts of your brain to understand. They are located directly behind the forehead and eyes, and they're the largest set of lobes in your brain. And guess what…they're much larger than the frontal lobes of most animals. The frontal lobes receive information from all the other lobes. They gather the information and put it together to allow us to respond to the world in a meaningful way. Our frontal lobes have *executive functions*, meaning they are where the supervision of many brain processes occurs. If you want a supervisor, this is the place to get one.

The good news is the frontal lobes help us anticipate the results of situations, plan our actions, initiate responses, and use feedback from the world to stop or change our behaviors. You can actually renew and change these lobes by focusing on positive statements. The bad news is this is where the groundwork for anxiety and worry lies.

This section is often a source of anxiety because these lobes anticipate and interpret situations, and anticipation often leads to anxiety. Anticipation can lead to another common process here that creates anxiety: worry. Because of our highly developed frontal lobes, humans have the ability to predict future events and imagine their consequences—unlike our pets, who seem to sleep peacefully without thinking about tomorrow's problems. Worry is an outgrowth of anticipation of negative outcomes in a situation.[8]

When you look at the future and ask, "What if...?" and answer it, that's worry. We have a built-in bent toward negative thinking. Especially when we've experienced painful upsets in our life.

Traumas can be remembered in the prefrontal part of the brain. Your neocortex is at work to remember important experiences in order to learn from the past for the purpose of making good decisions for the future. This is one of the important functions of this portion of your brain.

If you experienced a serious trauma, such as the shooting in Las Vegas or floods in Texas, you may remember what happened before and after the event but not the actual event itself, since your brain is saying, "I don't think I want to remember and experience this!"

When you send a healthy or positive memory to your executive portion or prefrontal and its accepted, it's more likely to look for this type of message and be more accepting of other messages that are similar. You may think, *Oh, this is just like that thing that happened before*, since this is an experience you filed away.

This is important to remember. For you to move forward you will need to turn off one section of your brain (the alarm and its painful memories) and turn on the neocortex frontal lobes.[9]

Our brains create explanations and then continue to look for them in other situations as a way of keeping us safe. We look for *safety.* Consider these experiences that plague many:

Abandonment: "I'll end up alone."

Deprivation: "My needs won't be met."

Subjugation: "It's always your way, not mine."

Mistrust: "They're out to get me."

Unlovability: "I'm not lovable."

Exclusion: "I'm always left out."

Vulnerability: "I'm responsible but can't control the situation, so I feel overwhelmed and worry excessively."

Failure: "I'm not good enough."

Entitlement: I'm special, so rules don't apply to me."

Perfection: "I have to do everything perfectly."

Who can live with these? Do you relate to any of these? If so, do you remember their origin?

We are emotional creatures. God created us and how we function. And the most amazing and perhaps least understood part of us is our brain. We may think, *I'm not influenced by my emotions that much. I'm a thinking, rational being.* That may be true, but our brain and mind are created in such a way that no information gets through to the rational thinking part without passing through the area of the brain where emotions originate. Emotions color that information and also determine how much attention is paid to it, whether we consciously acknowledge it or not.

When our emotional side (the right side of the brain) is highly activated, we tend to shut down the thinking or rational left side. It's like we're caught in an emotional grip or vise, but we insist that our thinking, even though highly influenced by our emotions, is accurate and logical, when in reality it might not be. Someone described this like his emotions had hijacked the rational side of his brain. No matter how much insight and understanding we develop, our rational, left side of the brain is basically needed to talk the emotional right brain out of its own reality.[10]

Has anyone ever said, "Quit responding with your emotions. Just think about this, and you'll respond better as well as calm down"? Does this work? No, it doesn't, and it won't.

Trauma impacts the brain when we experience an intense, unexpected event. It is as though it causes the left side (the cognitive or thinking side) and the right side (the emotional) to become disconnected from one another. Usually our body, emotions, and thoughts are all connected, but these kinds of events separate them.

Have you heard of *brain shifting*? Probably not. It occurs all the time, sometimes purposely and sometimes not. Brain scans have been used to help understand our functioning. Scans show that images of past trauma such as flashbacks activate the right side of our brain (the emotional or feelings side) and thoughts the left or thinking side. Each side of the brain speaks a different language.

Under ordinary circumstances the two sides of the brain work together more or less smoothly, even in people who might be said to favor one side over the other. However, having one side or the other shut down, even temporarily, or having one side cut off entirely (as sometimes happened in brain surgery) is disabling.

When you are traumatized and something reminds you of the past, your right brain reacts as if the traumatic event were happening right now, in the present. But because your left brain is not working very well, you may not be aware that you're reexperiencing and reenacting the past—you're furious, terrified, enraged, ashamed, or frozen. After the emotional storm passes, you may even look for something or somebody to blame for it. You think you behaved the way you did because of what someone else *did*. When you cool down, you hopefully can admit your mistake. However, trauma interferes with this kind of awareness.[11] Keep that in mind when the above happens. There's nothing wrong with you. It's the result of the unexpected.

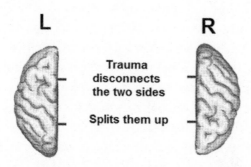

Your left brain and right brain have to pull together; otherwise just one side is in charge. That's not a real good situation. We may have vivid, graphic thoughts about what happened, but no emotion. It's like "Where did all my feelings go?" Or we may experience intense emotions without the thoughts or actual memories. Either way this is disturbing. As one man said, "I felt like my brain was disrupted, and one part transmitted on AM and the other on FM. Sometimes there are holes in my memory, like a slice was taken out. Other times I can't get those intrusive, unwanted memories to stop. I want them evicted! I can't remember what I want to remember and I can't forget what I want erased." The struggle is shared by many.[12] We're trying to cope with the unthinkable.

What happens when a threat is remembered? I've seen this first-hand with the victims of the Las Vegas shooting. I've seen their bodies tremble and their eyes glass over. Their nervous system is overly activated by the past threat. The event seems to continue to float free in time rather than have roots and stability. This event comes uninvited into the present and appears to the person as though it were happening now. I've seen this in their facial expressions.

Within the brain there are two related areas that are very important to the storage of memories. The *alarm section* is one, and the other portion is best described as your brain's *biographer* since it stores and retrieves conscious memories about what's going on now as well as events from the past and how you handled it and what happened. It's also called the hippocampus.[13]

The alarm section has a specific job. It processes the intense and emotionally charged memories such as terror and horror. On the other hand, the biographer puts memories in the proper perspective. It gives the proper time sequence to events such as a beginning, middle, and end. But when the alarm section is activated, the biographer's activity and functioning is diminished and the past traumatic event continues to involve the present.[14] It's as though that portion of your brain takes over.

Most change, negative or positive, has a companion—discomfort. One author said any change that is unasked for represents a death of some kind and is painful.

I like the phrase *uncharted waters*. We have a river not too far from where I live, and each year several people drown. They enter the water, but they don't know where the dangerous pools or submerged rocks are located. They're at risk since they don't know which section of the river is full of turbulence. They don't expect what they've run into.

Life is full of uncharted waters. Some people handle them well and some do not. Those who are flexible expect uncharted waters, and have the ability to adapt—not only to survive, but eventually thrive. They don't resist change but instead embrace it and use it. They are able to keep from getting stuck. Then there are those who do get stuck, and the results of being stuck are anger or bitterness, all of which are counterproductive. Resisting change tears us down and has a negative effect on our thinking process.[15]

Whatever you're going through right now and whatever this change means to you, there's always a sense of loss of control. When change comes from the outside, we aren't in charge of what's happening, and that's uncomfortable.[16] And what's worse is that when this happens, it causes us to feel unsafe. Has this been your experience? Probably so, for trauma destroys our feeling of safety.

Messages from the environment go to both the alarm portion and other parts of your brain, but *they always get to the alarm part faster.* That's why we *must* be more skillful at learning to interpret the messages. The trick is to use the logical part of your brain to convince the scared part of yourself that there is no danger, at least none that you can't deal with.[17]

> During a disaster, there is a phase where we delay action because we aren't sure whether we need to respond or what the right action might be. We mill around, our pattern-seeking brains trying to gather more data to make a decision.
>
> Milling causes delay. According to a National Institute of Standards and Technology survey, the average time before survivors evacuated at the World Trade Center on 9/11 was six minutes, and some people waited as long as forty-five minutes. Rather than just get out, people first called friends and family. Many even took the time to power down their computers.[18]

We need an emotional and cognitive helmet to protect our brain from disruption and concussion. Is there a part of your brain that helps you make decisions about right or wrong or good or bad or the consequences of your actions? Yes, there is, and it's important to access it and use it. It's been mentioned before, and it's called the prefrontal cortex—the executive section. It filters out what may be good or bad. But here's the problem: It's not working as well as it should when you experience the unexpected or a trauma, especially during the initial 48 hours. It's not running the show—the alarm section is in charge. A difference between the alarm section and your prefrontal is that they operate on different time tables.

This is where the emotional hijacking comes into play. The portion of our brain that is responsible for fear and anger is dominant.[19] So we need to access the prefrontal section.

Our brain generates emotions. We need these. And we were created as emotional beings. You're not limited emotionally, but you benefit from your emotions. But keep this in mind—when you are emotionally free rather than imprisoned you will have more resources to handle the difficult situations that occur.

Perhaps you're bound up because of what you experienced as a child, such as being told, "Don't cry," or "Stuff your feelings." You may have been damaged or hurt as a child emotionally and this hinders you. You have a choice—you can live in the past as a victim, or you can assume a new level of responsibility and take charge. People who do this are referred to as *overcomers*. Those who don't are in some ways prisoners in their own jail.

Emotions are part of our life. We need them—but in balance. Someone said emotion and reason work like a seesaw. The stronger your emotions, the more difficult it is to think clearly. But this is where the seesaw comes in. It can work the other way as well. If you're thinking straight, sometimes this process can override your emotions.

Where does this reasoning come in? Where else? In the front part of your brain, the frontal lobes. This is where restraining comes in too. The statements you make to yourself are the key. The more clearly you think, the more you can control the emotion that is so prevalent with these events...fear. [20]

Your brain is amazing. Do you know the brain can indeed be rewired? It can expand the area that is wired to move the fingers, forging new connections that underpin the dexterity of an accomplished violinist. It can activate long-dormant wires and run new cables like an electrician bringing an old house up to code so that regions that once saw can instead feel or hear. It can quiet circuits that once crackled with the aberrant activity that characterizes depression and cut pathological connections that keep the brain in the oh-God-something-is-wrong state that marks obsessive-compulsive disorder. The adult brain, in short, retains much of the plasticity of the developing brain, including the power to repair damaged regions, to grow new neurons, to rezone regions that performed one task and have them assume a new task, to change the circuitry that weaves neurons into the networks that allow us to remember, feel, suffer, think, imagine, and dream.[21]

I am working on my brain the older I get. I don't want my brain to either stagnate or deteriorate. There are so many books accessible today with games or exercises. Since I've played the piano for most of my life, I still play pieces that are quite easy for me. I don't have to think that much or work at the various numbers, so playing these is not really challenging pathways or creating new ones. Therefore I am purposely playing new styles such as music by Billy Joel, Louis Gottshock, Jerry Lee Lewis, and others. I can admit that some of these pieces are challenging, but they are also enjoyable. (I just can't stand up and kick my legs like Jerry.)

However, consider the following. How many minutes of each day of your life would you say are overtly negative, causing you intense emotional or physical pain or discomfort through new incoming experiences? This question doesn't include all the emotional and resultant physical suffering that gets provoked by your inner mind's ability to fixate on negative thoughts or worrying. We're talking about the percentage of your actual experiential day that hits you with decidedly negative encounters in the here and now. For many, it's a majority of the time.

In fact, most of our chronic moments emerge not from right here and now, but from our thinking minds dwelling on bad things that happened in the past to us, or imagining something anxiety provoking that might happen sometime in the future. The present moment is quite clearly our God-given haven from all such mentally generated suffering.[22] (It may help to read my book *A Better Way to Think*.)

Now, what can you do to get to the thinking part of your brain and let it be in charge?

Many go through life being controlled by the alarm section of their brain. And when I say controlled, that's exactly what I mean is happening, even though you may not be aware of it. The alarm portion or sentry is located in the middle of your brain, which means it gets information about threats very rapidly and sometimes even before the thinking part of your brain does.[23]

How can we switch to the CEO of our brain rather than allow our alarm section to control us? It's possible—read on.

There is good news about your brain. First of all, your brain can grow no matter how old you are. It can grow new positive pathways. It can help you see the upsets of life as challenges and thus calm down the alarm section of your brain. You don't need to be victimized by this section of your brain the rest of your life. Remember the alarm section reacts too fast, basically because of its location in your brain. It happens even before the thinking part of your brain can kick in.[24]

The portion of your brain that you want to access or be "in" is the CEO or the prefrontal cortex. This section is fairly large. It's here that some major responsibilities such as thinking and problem solving occur. It can hold in information about both your current situation *as well as* your past. It will process more information than your alarm section and thus make better and more informed choices.[25]

Once again let me ask the question: How can we switch to the CEO of our brain rather than allow our alarm section to control us?

The prefrontal cortex allows you to solve complex problems, control your impulses, calm down intense emotions, shift your attention, and adapt to new, uncertain, or changing situations. This part of your brain can help you suppress automatic fearful or angry responses to stressful situations so that you can respond more effectively.[26]

These are several suggestions of how you can do this:

The first is slow yourself down. Breathe in slowly and hold your breath for four or five seconds. You can do this whether you're at home or at the mall. Do this several times and you'll discover that you are more relaxed as well as thinking or moving at a different pace. When you hold your breath, your focus is no longer on the alarm or the pain or what has happened. Your breath is helping you relax, and your breath is helping you focus on the front part of your brain. Your entire body will begin to relax. Your alarm portion has a purpose to protect you. But when the unexpected occurs, it overreacts.

As you continue to breathe in and out, begin to repeat the following scriptures:

> You will keep in perfect peace those whose minds are steadfast, because they trust in you (Isaiah 26:3).

> ...to be made new in the attitude of your minds (Ephesians 4:23).

> Do not conform to the pattern of this world, but be transformed by the renewing of your mind. Then you will be able to test and approve what God's will is—his good, pleasing and perfect will (Romans 12:2).

> Therefore, with minds that are alert and fully sober, set your hope on the grace to be brought to you when Jesus Christ is revealed at his coming (1 Peter 1:13).

Your mind actually adapts to whatever you dwell upon.

There are numerous counseling approaches that are used to help overcome the results of being impacted by the unexpected. EMT or eye movement technique was originally used by a therapist and client in the counselor office but now is available for a person to use on his or her own. It is also called eye movement desensitization and reprocessing (EMDR). The procedure invades a rapid back-and-forth movement of the eyes or a tapping of the fingers. It has been used to reduce emotional stress from the past as well as the present-day issues, and redirects thinking as well as traumatic memories to be more positive and rational. This involves using more of the prefrontal part of the brain. One of the resources that will give you more information about this is *Do It Yourself Eye Movement Technique for Emotional Healing* by Fred Freiberg (New Harbinger Publishers, 2001). Before attempting to do this technique yourself, be sure to read page 2 of the recommended resource.

Another counseling approach that is quite effective is Thought Field Therapy (TFT). This can be used for problems identified previously under EMT. This has applications for a number of the traumatic stress responses. It appears to be a fast way of reducing stress that has lasting results. This approach uses a tapping technique or certain treatment points on the body. This does not take an excessive amount of time. I have seen this used in a class setting as well as a therapy situation, and the results were very positive. This approach is used to deal with memories and it also has an impact on intense emotions, especially fear. The tapping occurs on sites on the body where acupuncture points are used. Roger Callahan has done most of the work in this area, and his resource is *Stop the Nightmares of Trauma* by Roger J. Callahan and Joanne Callahan. Each of these approaches are worth pursuing.

Writing about painful experiences can be very helpful. Writing can help boost your immune system and keep your body healthy. Writing, like any form of expression, can be a healing activity. Writing about troubling experiences and the troubling aspects of your relationships helps you see them more clearly and gives you a sense of mastery over your experiences. Once you put something down on paper, you may make connections you were not previously aware of and you may get in touch with feelings you haven't experienced before.[27] You will find yourself shifting to the prefrontal portion.

Most who have experienced a trauma experience triggers or ambushes.

Many experience what we call hyperarousal. When I worked with victims of the Las Vegas shooting, I kept hearing how triggers were a part of their life, whether it be sights, sounds, crowds, shopping, smells, newscasts, etc. The author of *Trust After Trauma* describes what you may be experiencing:

> Even simple matters, such as standing in line in a store or picking out a movie, can be problematic. Life is harder for you than for someone who hasn't been traumatized because of all the triggers in your environment and within yourself. You may feel sad and angry that you have to work harder than most people just to get through the day and you are entitled to both of these feelings.
>
> There are many techniques that can help you manage and exert some control over your trigger reactions.[28]

The following exercise may be helpful. In your journal or on a piece of paper, write the following:

1. Triggers you feel might be the easiest to endure.
2. Triggers you feel you might be able to handle after a few more months of healing.
3. Triggers you feel you might be able to confront in a few years (maybe).
4. Triggers you plan to avoid for the rest of your life.

Then title a new page "Trigger Chart" and draw lines to make four columns. Label them, from left to right, "Easiest to Handle," "Possibly Manageable Within a Year," "Possibly Manageable in the Distant Future," and "Impossible to Ever Handle."

Now take your list from the first exercise and place each trigger in the appropriate category. All of these steps will bring you into the front portion of your brain.

When you feel ready to confront a trigger, select one from those you listed in column 1 of the Trigger Chart—a situation you judge one of the easiest to handle. Beginning with a more difficult trigger such as one in column 2 or 3 can be a setup for failure because no trigger situation, even one you classified as relatively easy to handle, is truly easy. You have to start somewhere, though, so it is best to start where you have the greatest chance of success.

Trigger Chart			
Easiest to Handle	Possibly Manageable Within a Year	Possibly Manageable in the Distant Future	Impossible to Ever Handle

Once you have completed this exercise, write out what you think you can do to handle these triggers. Find two safe people to share this with and discuss how they can help you at this time and how they can pray for you. Be honest about sharing your story and your feelings, and give as many details as possible. Go back to the chart to help you move forward.

One last thought about your body and especially your brain.

Consider your spinal column. The spine is made up of 33 bony pieces called vertebrae. These bones are stabilized by ligaments and separated by 23 intervertebral shock absorbers called discs. You have 6 discs in your neck, 12 in the middle of your back, and 5 in your lower back. This amazing design allows you to absorb the crushing blows your body experiences when running, jumping, or simply walking across a room. Without these shock absorbers, your back bones would slowly be crushed by pressure in the most common ritual of getting out of bed in the morning, let alone running a marathon or jumping in a gunny sack race on the Fourth of July. You were made to bounce. You were created with physical qualities that allow you to absorb the impact of shock and pressure without being crushed.

Your body also has the ability to heal itself. If you cut your hand, the wound will automatically begin to repair. This resilient healing process is constantly in motion in your body. It's what helps you rebound from wear and tear. Dying cells are replaced with new ones daily. Every 24 hours your body produces 200 billion new red blood cells. You feel refreshed after a good night's sleep, catch a second wind after a long day at work, and recover from a common cold or flu because your body is amazingly designed to bounce back.

We appreciate our bodies' resilience, especially when we suffer from an injury. But for the most part we are unaware of the awesome ability to repair going on under our skin. Have you ever wished your mind was created to be as resilient as your body? Wouldn't it be awesome if we could recover from life's crushing pressures and failures and bounce back the way our intervertebral discs do? When our life visions die, wouldn't it be comforting to know we can rejuvenate them the same way new red blood cells replace our dying ones?

The fact is, you were made to bounce back not only physically but also mentally, emotionally, and spiritually.

Think about your brain for a minute. You have 100 billion nerve cells called neurons in your brain. These neurons explode with electrical charges 300 billion times per second. And you wonder why you have mental fatigue after a long day at the office! These electrical charges are actually the makeup of our thoughts and words. Neurologists have discovered these electrical impulses form branches in our brains. They have found that healthy thoughts produce good trees and unhealthy thoughts produce bad trees. You could say these neuron trees are long-term memories.

Your brain was designed by a God of love, joy, and peace.[29]

CHAPTER 7

Terrorism

Terrorism—it's something we need to address since it's a part of our lives. We hear about it and use the term, but do we understand what it is? You and I are living with this problem, and it's not going to go away. As I write this I've spent the last month helping the victims of one of the worst attacks we've ever experienced that was carried out by what appears to have been a "lone wolf" terrorist. I listened to the stories until I couldn't listen anymore.

These are some of the responses of those who were terrorized:

- "I actually draped my body over the chaos to help my wife from the terrorist. People were dropping all around us and some never made it to safety."

- "I heard the gunfire, which I thought was fireworks. But it wasn't. It was one bullet after another. We were hit by whatever the ricochets were made of. I didn't know where the shots came from. I wanted my friends to be safe."

- "It was a war zone. I was in Iraq, and this was as bad or worse. The bullets were breaking into shrapnel. I still see this stuff and hear the sounds and see the images…and it's been months."

- "My daughter was on the floor, and I was next to her standing up. She looked up at me and reached her arm up to me, closed her eyes, and she was gone."

- "We called our children to tell them we loved them. They could hear the gunfire. We weren't sure we would see them again."

- "My husband was shot in the arm and the head. He died, but for hours we didn't know where his body was."

Story after story. Fifty-nine died and 527 were wounded. Several hundred had gone to the Route 91 Harvest Festival from the area where I live, and I sat with many of the survivors for weeks.

A theme I heard was "I've never been so scared! I don't know if I'll ever feel safe again." I saw bodies tremble and shake, and heard individuals describe how they felt.

I wasn't there during the shooting, yet in many ways I feel like I was. I lived through it as I sat with the victims, many of whom were present during the attack. Others had loved ones who had run for their life, stumbling over bodies already dead or in the process of dying. I can still see the eyes of the nurse who said it was the worst war zone she had ever seen or of the young bride who pointed to the two wounds she had received. I heard person after person try to describe the horror they experienced. My heart went out to the couple who left the debriefing because it was so painful. They lost their adult daughter. Since I've lost both of my children, I do understand, and sometimes the pain of others activates mine again even after all these years. As I hear the stories I realize it will take years for many to grieve, to feel safe again, and to experience the joy that has been diminished by this event.

Then, as if this weren't enough, another slaughter occurred a month later when a lone gunman entered a church service in the small town of Sutherland, Texas. He was angry and chose to take out his anger that Sunday morning on the congregation. Twenty-six people were killed and 20 wounded when he entered the church randomly firing multiple rounds of ammunition.

Just think about the other events that have occurred during the fall of 2017. These are just the tip of the iceberg. (By the time this book is released who knows what else might have happened.)

So, what is terrorism? Ask the average person on the street, and you'll get a wide variety of responses. It's not an ideology like communism or capitalism. There is a specific end goal in the mind of the terrorist, and he or she believes terrorism is how to get there.

Terrorism is by nature a mind game. Terrorists understand the experience of dread that they try to create. It's one of the best ways to get people agitated.[1] They use fear to take away our sense of safety.

One of the oldest professions in the world is combatting terrorism. Even before the first century, governments have struggled successfully to handle terrorism.

For every successful intervention to deal with this problem there have been a far greater number of terrorists who were successful in carrying out their attacks. Trying to deal with individual or lone-wolf terrorists and control the problem can be overwhelming since they can do their work anywhere and any time. It's impossible to protect every target all the time.[2]

What is it? Terrorism is an extremely complex set of phenomena, covering a great diversity of groups with different origins and causes. We're going to look at this in detail since its presence is here and will intensify.

So, to identify the root causes of terrorism is a complex task for several reasons. The many failed attempts to find one common definition of terrorism have been frustrated by the fact that the label *terrorism* is used to cover a wide range of responses and approaches. Rebellious groups and powerful states may both use terrorist methods to intimidate target groups, but the nature of "terror from above" (committed by the government) and "terror from below" (committed by individuals) differs in several fundamental ways.

Are we really safe? Perhaps not. Terrorism has been with the world around us for centuries. Its roots and practices came from the first-century zealots. Finally, it's arrived on our shores. And so now our country as we know it has changed. We've been invaded not by a foreign army or swarms of biologically altered swarms of insects, but by something that is more deadly—terrorism.

Terrorists intentionally use violence to disrupt our lives, and it doesn't take many events to disrupt us, dominate our thinking, and take away our sense of safety. This is at the heart of what they do…steal our sense of safety from us. They strike where we least suspect their presence. They plant the seeds of suspicion and paranoia. We tense up when we board a plane or walk through the doors of a subway train or enter the doorway of a church.

We wonder about things we never thought of ten years ago. The phrase *what if…* floods our mind.

Just recently I spoke at a church for their worship service. A gentleman came up and sat next to me and said, "I'm part of the security force for the church. There's another armed man behind the curtain behind you. We will respond to a shooter if we need to." I have to admit as I walked up to the stage and the pulpit I looked the audience over carefully. I found out later there were eight security guards scattered amongst the congregation.

When a terrorist attacks, and we can expect more, our lives are disrupted, not just for months but for decades.

> Each new cycle of terrorism brings with it remnants from the past. We have not seen the last of major hijackings, bombings or hostage taking terrorism. No other form of violence approaches the mystery and uniqueness of terrorism. For the relatively simple act of hijacking a plane, or kidnapping a person, or blowing up a building, a whole sequence of global events can unfold that can last months, years or even decades beyond that brief moment of violence.[3]

Terrorism is a conflict based on political, economic, and social grievances that can never be fully resolved. There have been and there are basic causes for terrorist activity, and they are not going to change. Those who want a cause will find it. Terrorist groups and terrorist lone wolves will be on the rise since technology is becoming refined. As one specialist said, "We can expect another cycle of terrorism in the years ahead. Several trends point to future terrorist environment that will be unlike any we have experienced."[4]

And it's not just the victims and their families who are impacted; everyone is. That may sound like an overreaction, but with the media and its immediate and prolonged coverage and posting of videos on the internet, no one can escape the impact. And all of this puts pressure on the government to respond and "do something" about them. We also find politicians who make use of the events for their own advantage.

The mass media has also made it more difficult for the president of our country and what he can accomplish. Unfortunately, terrorists have made use of various media for their own advantage. Because we stay fixated and addicted to the news programs and social media, we respond emotionally and emails and tweets exert pressure on the leadership of our country.[5] Individuals and groups want action, and they want their voice heard.

Terrorists are the perpetrators of a violent incident. Some feel that to cause terror with a violent event is a justifiable act of war against an oppressive opponent. They do this to attract attention. In their minds this is a legitimate tactic because from their point of view, many feel they are freedom fighters, not terrorists.

Terrorist violence can be used to spin incidents so that they symbolize punishment or chastisement against victims for injustices the terrorists feel they have suffered. From the terrorists' point of view, high-profile attacks that victimize an audience are useful as "wake-up calls" for the victims to understand the underlying grievances of the movement the terrorists say they are fighting for.

Terrorists are proud of their attack and want to draw attention to their exploits.

Targets are often symbolic victims. They represent some feature of the enemy and can be either property targets or human targets. As is the case with the victim, human targets will rarely sympathize with the terrorists. If they are looking for support, they won't receive it.[6]

Tactically successful terrorist events are rare occurrences, but they represent the tip of an iceberg when it comes to all planned attacks. Most attacks planned by terrorists fail for reasons internal to the plot or they are stopped by external intervention. For example, in the past 15 years since the 9/11 attacks, there have been around a hundred jihadist-linked plots to attack American targets in the United States, but only eight of those plots resulted in the deaths of their intended victims. Were you aware of this? Most of us aren't. There are many other non-jihadist individual or group attacks.

You may be shocked at some of these numbers. One of the most surprising statistics is that many of the recorded terrorist attacks do *not* result in fatalities. Of the nearly 156,772 attacks in the database through 2015, only 51 percent (79,411 attacks) resulted in at least one fatality. For more than 49 percent of attacks the media sources we use to record cases did not report any deaths.[7]

The Ten Deadliest Attacks Against US Territory, 1970–2018

Rank	Year	Location	Fatalities
1	2001	New York City	2,763
2	2001	Arlington, Virginia	189
3	1995	Oklahoma City, Oklahoma	168
4	2017	Las Vegas, Nevada	59
5	2016	Orlando, Florida	49
6	2001	Shanksville, Pennsylvania	44

7	2017	Sutherland Springs, Texas	26
8	2018	Parkland, Florida	17
9	2015	San Bernardino, California	16
10	1999	Littleton, Colorado	15[8]

Researchers have identified more than 200 definitions of terrorism but have failed to agree on any one, and the idea that one person's terrorist is another person's freedom fighter has become cliché.[9]

Let's consider the terms *terrorism* and *terrorist*. The strategy of a terrorist is often used when a weaker person or group is fighting against something or someone more powerful. The violence is aimed at creating fear in others and often provokes a prompt and violent response in return. In fact, acts of terrorism followed by violent responses can become a cycle that is difficult to break.

Just recently terrorist groups and factions have started using the internet and media to create fear and impact public opinion or recruit followers. And it's not just small groups, but nations also use tactics of terrorism in other countries to safeguard their own national interests.

Is there any way to really know what terrorists want? Terrorists are not all after the same thing. They often justify their bloody acts on the basis of what they see as unfairness, or their cause could be social or political. Or they could be basing their attacks on religious or spiritual beliefs. When you study the history of this problem, you find that many forms of terrorism were inspired by warfare between races, conflicts between the rich and poor, or political outcasts.

Many terrorist groups are inspired by their interpretation of religious teaching or prophetic scriptures. I'm sure you've heard of Al-Qaeda and ISIS. These are two related groups that justify their violent actions as part of their crusade on those they label as nonbelievers.

Terrorism carried out in the name of faith has long been a feature of human affairs. During the Middle Ages, the Western Christian (or Roman Catholic) church launched at least nine invasions of the Islamic east, the first one in 1095. These invasions were termed *Crusades* because they were conducted in the name of the cross. Basically, the purpose of the Crusades was to capture the holy lands from the disunited Muslims, whom they referred to collectively as Saracens.

Christian knights and soldiers answered the call for many reasons. The promise of land, riches, and glory were some of the main reasons. Another important reason was the spiritual promise, made by Pope Urban II, that fighting and dying in the name of the cross would ensure martyrdom and thereby guarantee a place in heaven. Freeing the holy lands would bring eternal salvation. Thus, "knights who with pious intent took the Cross would earn a remission from temporal penalties for all his sins; if he died in battle he would earn remission of his sins."[10]

Not all Christian Crusades were fought in Muslim lands. The Western church also purged its territories of Jews and divergent religious beliefs that were denounced as heresies. A careful study of the various crusades today would lead us to say that terrorism was rampant during these centuries.

What about terrorism and religious faith?

The histories of people, civilizations, nations, and empires are filled with examples of extremist "true believers" who engaged in violence to promote their particular belief system. Some religious terrorists are inspired by defensive motives; others do this to ensure the predominance of their faith.

Is there any difference between faith-based terrorism and non-faith terrorism? No. Faith-based violence exhibits the same qualities as other terrorist responses. Terrorism can be communal, genocidal, nihilistic, or revolutionary. It can be committed by lone wolves, cell groups, large dissident movements, or even governments. And depending on one's perspective, there is often debate about whether the perpetrators should be classified as terrorists or religious freedom fighters.

Within the Jewish-Christian belief system, there are references in the Bible not only to assassinations and conquests but also to the complete destruction of enemy nations in the name of the faith. One such campaign, you might remember, is described in the book of Joshua.

The story of Joshua's conquest of Canaan is the story of the culmination of the ancient Hebrews' return to Canaan. To Joshua and his followers, this was the "promised land" of the covenant between God and the chosen people. This was in keeping with God's will and plan. According to Scripture, the Canaanite cities were destroyed and the Canaanites themselves were attacked until "there was no one left who breathed."[11] Assuming that Joshua and his army put to the sword all the inhabitants of the 31 cities mentioned in the Bible, and assuming that each city averaged 10,000 people, his conquest cost 310,000 lives.[12] The conquering of this land was according to God's will and purpose, which is far different than what is occurring today.

In Europe, countries that endured terrorist campaigns have written official definitions of terrorism.[13]

Terrorists attacks have these three common characteristics:

1. They are violent, or they threaten violence. The more, the better.

2. They are designed to coerce or intimidate a certain population of people (i.e., citizens or government, any noncombatants).

3. They are motivated by an ideology (political, religious, etc.)

Even with these three elements, there are many attacks, like some mass shootings, that fall within a gray area because they don't fit the stereotypical idea of a terrorist attack.

For example, in July of 2011, a man opened fired in a movie theater, killing 12 people and injuring another 70. He wanted to kill as many as possible that day and said that homicide was his way of dealing with his depression. He considered this to be a better option than suicide. While his actions were undoubtedly very violent, and many terrorists have committed mass shootings, his actions do not make him a terrorist. This attack was not driven by any sort of political or religious ideology, and he wasn't trying to coerce any action from the government or citizens; he did it simply *because he wanted to.*

Consider this phrase mentioned earlier: "One person's terrorist is another person's freedom fighter."

Our country was founded by many who today might be considered terrorists. The Sons of Liberty were organized during the American Revolution. You may have heard of them in your American history class. They wanted independence from Britain. They used violence in the 13 colonies to gain their freedom. They protested to the extent of tar and feathering supporters of the British Crown. There were two perspectives of this group.

From the colonists' point of view, they were fighting for their rights and freedom. Britain saw it differently—they saw the uprisers as terrorists. The colonists used violence as well as threats of violence. They were trying to influence and coerce Britain. The colonists saw their motives as positive. Britain thought otherwise. So were they terrorists or not? Perspective plays a role here.[14]

What about hate crimes? Are they acts of terrorism? The answer is that not all acts of terrorism are hate crimes, and not all hate crimes are acts of terrorism.

A number of terrorism experts have given us this definition: It's the illegitimate use of force to achieve a political objective when innocent people are targeted. It's a strategy of violence designed to promote desired outcomes by instilling fear in the public at large.

The use of threat or force is designed to bring about some type of change. When we look at the common features of terrorism:

- Illegal force is used.
- Unconventional methods are often employed.
- Political motives could be involved or it could be a hate crime.
- Some will be attacks against civilians or passive military targets.
- The acts are aimed at purposefully affecting an audience.[15]

Loosely defined, terrorism is the use of violence with the aim of furthering a political or ideological goal at the expense of the general population. Terrorism can take many forms and has many causes, often more than one.

Some terrorist events are singular acts linked to a particular historical moment, such as the assassination of Austria's Archduke Franz Ferdinand in 1914, which touched off World War I. Other terrorist attacks are part of an ongoing campaign that may last years, or even generations, as was the case in Northern Ireland from 1968 to 1998.

When you look at the history of terrorism, it's rare that there was a time when it wasn't occurring.

Although acts of terror and violence have been committed for centuries, terrorism's modern roots can be traced to the French Revolution's Reign of Terror in 1793–94. Between 17,000 to 40,000 people were executed by guillotine.

The type of acts and purposes seem to have expanded year after year. Even animal rights groups have begun to use terrorism. And now members of some groups such as ISIS use social media to further its cause.

As I've sat with the victims of terrorism in Colorado, Southern California, and Las Vegas, I've both seen and heard the changes stemming from the shootings. I've seen intense fear and anxiety in victims. Predictors of lasting effects include being closer to the attacks, being injured, or knowing someone who was killed or injured. Those who watch more media coverage are also at higher risk for PTSD and associated problems. So many who were at the Las Vegas shooting watched the videos on Facebook and then wondered why they couldn't sleep.

Terrorism steals the sense of safety away from people. I heard this time and time again from victims of every shooting and disaster that I've counseled. Feeling safe gives us security and comfort and when safety is part of our life, fear diminishes and we can be productive. Terrorism takes away our need to see the world as predictable, orderly, and controllable. Research shows that deliberate violence creates longer lasting mental health effects than natural disasters or accidents. However, for most, symptoms of fear, anxiety, reexperiencing, avoidance, and hyperarousal will gradually decrease over time.

What have we learned about the effects of terrorism?

We find that since the 9/11 attack, there has been an increasing amount of research about how people are affected by terrorism. While most individuals exhibit resilience over time, people most directly exposed to terrorist attacks are at higher risk for developing PTSD.[16] They are traumatized. I've seen them and sat with them. I've shared their pain with them.

Trauma continues long after the danger is gone. The victims relive the event as though it were continuing in the present. Time seems to stop. They're never sure the danger is really gone. This can continue for years.

When trauma hits, you no longer have a balance in your life. Either you have bouts of amnesia or you are constantly living the event. You're overrun by emotions or there's no feeling at all. That's what a terrorist act creates.

Most people resort to terrorism for three major reasons:

Politics is one. People choose terrorism when they are trying to right what they perceive to be a social, political, or historical wrong.

Another is religion. We've seen a number of attacks carried out in the name of religion.

Then there are the socioeconomic reasons. There are numerous forms of deprivation that can drive people to terrorism, in particular, poverty, lack of education, or lack of political freedom. Can you think of any examples?

If you look at any group that is widely understood as a terrorist group, you will find these elements are basic to their story.

What makes terrorism possible? What is a terrorist like? Who is most likely to become a terrorist?

Some are motivated by the circumstances they live in, such as political or social repression, or economic strife.

Terrorism is not simple. It is a complex phenomenon; it is a specific kind of political violence committed by people who do not have a legitimate army at their disposal. There is nothing inside any person or in their circumstances that send them directly to terrorism that we know of. We do realize that our fallen nature, sin, and evil in this world all come into play. For the terrorist certain conditions make violence against civilians seem like a reasonable and even necessary option.[17] Their thinking differs from ours.

> The basic causes of terrorism will remain unchanged in the coming years. The pursuit of territory, power, ideology, religion, revenge, and personal greed will continue to motivate individuals, groups and governments to commit terrorist acts. Some terrorist groups will also seek to exploit conditions of poverty, socioeconomic frustration, and political alienation in various countries in order to win sympathy among the masses.

> Since technology will continue to march forward along with the various conflicts of the world, we can expect another cycle of terrorism in the years ahead. Several

trends point to future terrorist environment that will be unlike any we have experienced.[18]

So far terrorists have tended to concentrate on seven basic types of tactics: hijackings, kidnappings, bombings, assassinations, armed assaults, barricade-hostage incidents, and produce contamination. Bombings have been one of the most favored.

What can we expect for the future? There will be a proliferation of high-tech weapons. Just think of the various delivery systems such as drones!

There are also weapons of mass destruction including nuclear bombs, chemical agents, and biological agents, to name a few.

Why would terrorists resort to using these? Simply because what has been used before isn't enough to achieve the end result they are looking for. These will have a greater impact as well as increase the number of casualties. You may be thinking either this possibility is scary or that this will never occur here. It's yes to both. It is scary to think about, and yes, it can happen here. Just remember the Twin Towers and 9/11.[19]

We now have the phrase "lone wolf terrorist."

Lone wolf terrorists can come from all walks of life. They are unpredictable as well. The internet will be used more and more by them. All it takes is one attack like the one in Las Vegas or Sutherland Springs, Texas, to throw our nation into fear.

> Lone wolves have also demonstrated that they can have a profound effect on governments and societies. In the United States, Timothy McVeigh changed the way many Americans viewed terrorism with just one major attack in Oklahoma City, making people realize that homegrown American terrorists were as serious a threat as Islamic and other foreign-based extremists.

The combination of danger, innovation and impact that has characterized lone wolf terrorism in the past is destined to continue in the future. So, too, will the effort by governments and law enforcement to design ways to effectively combat this threat. While many lone wolf attacks, like those initiated by terrorist groups, will not be that significant in terms of the damage they cause or the reactions they elicit, others will undoubtedly have serious effects.[20]

Unfortunately, it is the lone wolf operatives who usually are the most creative in terms of what they do and how they do it. They are actually introducing new ways to attack, and other terrorist groups are learning from what they have done.[21] They work alone so they don't have to obtain the consensus of a group. They have free reign.

Remember the impact of the President Kennedy assassination? One person's action impacted the entire world. We lost our innocence because of this political violence. The image of what had been built up while Kennedy was in office came crashing down. And it didn't stop with Kennedy's assassination. A few years later we were shocked once again by the actions of one person when Martin Luther King and Robert Kennedy were killed. Our country was just as vulnerable as anywhere else.[22]

The world of lone wolf terrorism will continue to evolve in the coming years. We cannot predict the new issues that may arise to propel certain people into terrorism. It could be global economic and political developments, certain policies by various governments, or just a local issue that angers a particular individual. But whatever the cause, the lone wolf will try to remain anonymous and in the background until he or she strikes. Uncovering the secret world of the lone wolf terrorist will remain one of the major challenges in the battle against this form or terrorism.[23]

Part of the problem is the availability of technology, namely the internet. Just think about this: One person (a lone terrorist) can learn all they need to know about weapons, how to construct explosives, and the steps to take to build a homemade biological weapon. Let's think about the internet and what possibilities are available.

Jeffrey Simon, author of the book *Lone Wolf Terrorism*, described the problem:

> The most important aspect of the Technological Wave that helps explain the growing prominence of the lone wolf terrorist is the Internet. In fact, the Internet can be considered the grand event that helped launch the wave.
>
> By the first decade of the twenty-first century, the Internet was an integral part of everyday life for many people. One could find information on virtually any topic and feel connected to the world at large with a laptop computer or a smartphone. For the individual interested in perpetrating a terrorist attack, everything from how to build homemade bombs to maps and diagrams of potential targets were available on the Internet. So, too, were detailed accounts of terrorist incidents around the world, which lone wolves could study in order to determine what might work for them. In addition, the Internet provided a mechanism for lone wolves to become infatuated with extremist ideologies through the reading of websites, blogs, Facebook pages, and other tools available online. Lone wolves could also find other like-minded individuals on the Internet and obtain help from one or two other people in perpetrating an attack.

The Internet also provides lone wolves with an easy means for conducting surveillance of potential targets, including detailed maps of airports and buildings, flight and train schedules, and even computer images of the inside of a specific plane, indicating how many passengers will be on a flight and the exact location of available seats.[24]

How can we explain the rise in lone wolf terrorism? The technology necessary for terrorists to carry out their attacks is becoming more and more accessible. Whatever a terrorist wants to know about technology that can be used for terrorist activity can be found on the internet, whether it's how to build a bomb or the highest velocity bullet. The use of the internet is indispensable. For example, two of the resources found on the internet are *The Terrorist Handbook* and *How to Make a Bomb, Book 2*.

There are numerous events that qualify for the designation "lone wolf terrorism." It usually involves only one or two individuals. They usually work without the assistance from anyone else, and they can devastate a large group of people and strike fear into not just our country but to all those adjacent to us.

Are all lone wolf terrorists the same? If not, how can you distinguish them? Perhaps it's what motivates them or what drives them and their purpose that makes them distinct. One type is the person who commits his acts for political or a separatist cause. An example of this is Timothy McVeigh, who blew up the Federal Building in Oklahoma City in 1995 and killed 168 people.

Another type is the lone wolf who attacks in the name of religions, whether it is Christianity, Islam, or white supremacy.

A third type commits an attack because of a specific issue, whether that's abortion or the environment or animal rights.

The fourth type is motivated by the financial rewards.

The fifth group is those who are driven by personality and psychological problems.[25]

There are overlaps of the different types.

This threat has emerged as one of the "most bewildering, frustrating and dangerous forces of violence of our times."[26]

Large conspiracies are easier to identify and uncover. It's the lone individual that is much more difficult to detect.

> The diversity in lone wolf terrorism also means that, just like terrorism overall, it can never truly be "defeated." As long as there are individuals and groups who believe that terrorism is justified in the name of some cause, we will always have terrorism.[27]

For example, Timothy McVeigh blew up the Federal Building in Oklahoma City because he was angry at the US government for all the deaths at the Branch Davidian Cult headquarters. It was his anger that motivated him.

It's not just the deaths that occur from these events that do damage; there is ongoing damage to family members, first responders, rescue workers, and the entire city itself. For years I've had a picture on my desk of a fire fighter carrying an infant out of the rubble. This rescue worker never recovered from what he saw and experienced and years later took his life.

This danger will continue to grow in the future.

> For the surviving victims of terrorist incidents and the families of those killed by terrorists, the emotional scars will last a lifetime. The heart-wrenching cellular phone calls that some of the passengers on the doomed jets made to loved ones will haunt those relatives forever. The public also feels the emotional impact of terrorism, as each new incident heightens the fear of being the next victim. It may take a long time before people feel safe again about boarding an airplane. And in this age of extensive media coverage of terrorist events, we all

vicariously live through the pain and suffering of the victims and their families. It was therefore not surprising to find an overwhelming expression of public grief and sorrow over the tragedy...

The image of this country's military and financial centers being struck with such devastating force by terrorists, and the loss of so many innocent lives, will be etched in the minds of all Americans for many years to come.[28]

P.S. As I reread this chapter, I reflected on the past week, when 17 students were killed at a high school by a shooter and a bomb went off at a New York subway with casualties, and there were other events. What else will occur?

CHAPTER 8

Tell Me Your Story

W e all have a life story. But it is often disrupted by the unexpected. When this occurs, our story is like a novel that has lost one of the main characters before the story ends. As the future chapters are written and unfold, somehow we have to make sense of the disruption and create new chapters. This may involve some new characters as well as a revised plot that brings back meaning to the story.

The question arises, "How can we establish the plot of the original story after such disruption?"

Perhaps it's best to do so by simply telling and retelling the story to those who listen and care. My favorite words I share with those I counsel are, "Tell me your story." I don't say it once but many times.

Stories put confusion in order and meaning to what seems empty. Often within the story numerous questions are raised like, "What was the cause of this?" or "Where is the meaning in this?"

Telling our stories can help us to find ourselves and support.[1]

WHY SHOULD YOU TELL YOUR STORY?

For many it's tempting to leave barriers in place about what happened in their life. Like sandbags in a flood, they keep the murky waters of pain away from our hearts. So why would anyone want to remove the sandbags and let the waters flow in? Isn't that just too risky and maybe even foolish?

First, we tell our stories because the event won't go away by itself. The waves may recede like floodwaters, but like floodwaters, they leave a path of hurt and destruction. They leave us feeling confused and broken inside, and all the pain doesn't just disappear—even with good advice and "biblical information."

One of the survivors from the high school shootings at Columbine offered wise advice to the Virginia Tech and Colorado Springs survivors:

> For those of us who openly shared our thoughts, who cried, and who dealt with the pain immediately after it happened, we're not doing too bad. It still hurts, I still find occasion to cry. But those who never dealt with it find themselves unable to handle the simplest things. A fire alarm goes off, a balloon pops, or a police car drives by, and they find themselves doubled over in anguish, unable to move…We all deal with these things in different ways…It doesn't matter how we deal with it—as long as we do.[2]

There's a second important reason to tell our story: Sharing the story starts the healing process. On one level, sharing your story will "lift the veil" of denial, mystery, and silence that so often shrouds the event.

Telling the story helps validate you and your perspective. The recent events you experienced—the sights, sounds, feelings, smells—can seem like the random jumble of an automobile junkyard. By sharing the story, you can start to organize the jumble of sensations, making sense out of the senselessness of it all. You also start to break the grip of denial and set your heart free to face the truth—in all its jagged beauty and pain.

There is a simple power in telling our stories "on our own terms."

There are at least three levels to sharing our story of past trauma. First, there is the heart level. We simply acknowledge to ourselves that we're carrying pain from past events.

We've developed sophisticated mechanisms to hold the pain at bay, but the pain keeps oozing around our defensive walls. At this level, we're simply honest about this fact.

At this stage there is a temptation to say, "I should be better. I should be further along. I should move beyond the trauma, so I'll pretend or hope that things are better." One big "should" regarding healing is that we should not ask for help.

Second, once we stop running into defenses and attend to our heart, we can move into the next level of getting our story out: We become totally honest with God.

Jesus is not the kind of High Priest who will say, "Get over it! Haven't you dealt with that by now? What's taking you so long? And by the way, it didn't really hurt that bad, did it?" No, when Jesus looked at the crowds of hurting people, "He felt compassion for them, because they were distressed and dispirited like sheep without a shepherd" (Matthew 9:36 NASB). On the long road to recovering from past events, Jesus joins us as our caring older brother (Hebrews 2:11) and as our merciful High Priest who can "sympathize with our weaknesses" (Hebrews 4:15 NASB).

Third, as we begin to tell our story to our own heart and in the presence of God, we can move to the last level of getting the story out: We find safe people who will listen to our story.

Telling your story will help you make sense of what happened to you as well as help your brain heal. What you have experienced is probably stuck in both the left and right side of your brain. Each side responds in a different way with a story. Your right side is the picture side. It processes visual and spatial information. What you find here is autobiographical information, nonverbal information, intense emotion pictures, and social information. But your left side involves logic and language-based processing. This is the side that has words. It tries to relate how the unexpected event makes sense. As you tell the story, your right and left side of the brain begin to work together so the insightful and reflective parts of your brain are engaged. A sense of time now begins to make sense. You've read about this in the chapter on the brain.

A number of studies tell us why stories are important. We know that stories

- are universal.
- are found throughout the human life span, playing an important role in intergenerational relationships.
- involve logical sequencing of events but also play a powerful role in regulating emotions (in this way stories are good examples of how emotional and analytical thinking are intertwined).
- play a role in everyday communication as well as in the internal sense of who we are.
- play a vital role in memory processes.
- have been correlated with brain function, particularly since the left hemisphere is driven to make logical sense while the right hemisphere supplies the emotional context and autobiographical data needed for a personal story to make sense.[3]

If the unexpected event has impacted an entire family or a group, it's important for each person to be able to tell their story.

Simply telling the story, recounted in a safe and secure environment, gives victims the sense of being helped in their distress. They're not healing alone. The storytelling allows painful and powerful thoughts and feelings to be externalized in a way that rapidly reduces the power and pain of what happened. A collective sharing of the story, with participation from all involved in the crisis, validates individual experience and sensitizes each person to the unique experience of other members.[4]

If you try to handle it alone, you could end up being stuck. And when you hear others share, you realize that you are not alone in your experience. They are struggling as you are.[5]

The experience of the unexpected will always elicit a knot of painful and distressing symptoms. A powerful element to being the healing process is to invite all members of the experience—direct and indirect victims and caregivers—to share their individual and collective stories.

It helps if you can assist others with their storytelling and sharing in a way that will progressively bring more of the details of the experience to light. When you receive help, it encourages each person's progressive feeling of being understood and heard, which is so important, for it develops and deepens understanding.

This storytelling process may be repeated numerous times as the victims search for ways to integrate experiences that have no place in their mind and functioning. One person explained it this way: "It is like an old-fashioned flour sifter. To get the flour to the right consistency, you have to turn the sifter over and over and over until it eventually is all sifted through." In telling your story, you're able to gradually make an alien experience make sense.

Many survivors have an intense need to share the story of what happened to them. As we said before, telling your story validates you because when you tell another person your story, you are telling the world, "This awful thing happened to me. It truly happened, and it has affected me ever since." It's a message that needs a voice. And all it takes is one person listening to help bring comfort.

Often we fear that telling will alienate or emotionally disturb others, or that others will judge us harshly for our actions during the trauma or see us as deficient human beings because we happened to be caught in a trauma.

Telling the story to someone sometimes is an imperative. Keep this thought in mind: You survived to tell the story, and you may need to tell the story to survive. Telling your story helps you organize the chaos of the experience and know yourself. And you may need to tell your story many times in order to remember the details and to make sense of what happened, as well as to understand how the different people and events in your trauma relate to one another. I've listened to the same story from numerous individuals, and I've seen them change and transition. This was part of the healing.

Initially telling your story may set off a trigger or retraumatize you. Nevertheless, in the long run, telling your story can help desensitize you to the trauma.

If you were traumatized, you lived through a great drama. However, unless you were very fortunate, you probably had no place to talk about it. Who was safe? You, as a trauma survivor, need a place to speak the truth of what happened to you. Telling your story—under the right conditions—helps to detoxify any shame and guilt you may feel and, as such, empowers you and others.

There is a common misconception that "getting it all out" or "sharing all your secrets" will cure you.

In fact, talking extensively about your trauma when you are still being overwhelmed by the feelings associated with it could cause you to regress and develop even more distress symptoms than you already have.

In general, it's not wise to tell your story to someone you just met or whom you don't know very well, even though you may have a strong impulse to do so.

During your trauma, you had no or little control. You couldn't stop anything. But when telling your story, you can change the subject whenever you feel the need. But just because you may feel like telling your story doesn't mean you have to act on that feeling.

Also, once you start sharing it, you can stop telling your story whenever you want, at any place. Just because you begin with the intention to tell the whole tale does not mean you have to complete it.

Stop if you find yourself being triggered by your story into a state of upset or hyperarousal or any of the other conditions you may have struggled with. If this occurs, you could say, "I want to share with you, but I find myself becoming too upset, so I'm going to have to stop for now. The fact that I stopped telling my story to you has nothing to do with you. It's because I'm becoming overwhelmed. Thank you for listening as much as you did. Maybe I can finish my story another time."

You can even ask your listener how he or she is feeling or reacting, or whether he or she is willing to listen to more or wants you to stop.

In the past, part of your being upset may have been because of the fact that you could not talk about your experience. You might have been warned not to say anything, or you may have known that if you did speak up, you would be punished or hurt.

It is also important, however, not to let your fears about what might happen determine your decision about telling your story. Remember, you don't have to tell all your story. You can share in a general way or share only those aspects you feel are suitable to the situation and safe for you to disclose.

The following exercise may help you. It's designed to help you understand the consequences of telling your story. It may help to use a journal with a lock on it just to keep you safe.

Your story has many parts and many levels. Telling your story doesn't mean sharing every aspect of it with everyone. You can decide in advance what parts of your story you feel comfortable about sharing and what parts you want to keep to yourself. These questions may help you:

1. Are there parts of your story you don't want to share with anyone? What are those parts?

2. Are there parts of your story you would share only with a counselor or a best friend or partner, but no one else?

3. Have you shared your story in the past? Looking back on the times you shared your story, what do you wish you had done differently?

4. Consider three people in your life today with whom you would like to share your story or more of your story.

Before you begin to write in your journal, take a few minutes to think about where and when you would like to tell your story.

1. How can you set the time and the place and other aspects of the situation for telling your story so that you can increase your chance of being truly heard?

2. An alternative way to tell your story is to describe the specific events only in the most general terms and focus your account on what your feelings were during the trauma.

3. Now, do some writing about how you can tell your story in terms of *feelings*, rather than details of the events. Add to this writing your thoughts about how you can tell your story in terms of the kinds of struggles you have in your daily life today.[6]

Your reaction to what you have written may be mixed. You may want to reject and discard it. You may want to rewrite it again and again to fill in the gaps, or you may feel you've overdone it and written a book. The goal is to get every bit of it out of you and onto the paper.

If this experience is overwhelming, you may need to work at it in pieces and put it aside at times. And yet healing comes through the process of facing the pain and reconstructing the story.[7]

Often the reconstruction of the story can make you more aware of what you've lost, which may put you into a deeper sense of mourning. But this is an opportunity for recovery.

The next step is perhaps best thought of as an evaluation of how the trauma has impacted your life. How did this event change you? Challenge you? What did it do to your values and beliefs? How did this event affect your relationships?

One of the purposes of telling and retelling your trauma story is to lessen the intense feelings and eventually see it fade like other memories. It no longer is as significant as it was, and you no longer refer to yourself as a traumatized person.[8]

It's important to continue writing. And now it's no longer about the past but your future—what you want it to be and who you want to be. It's time to reconnect with life. Old beliefs, ways of responding, and a new outlook can be developed to replace the discarded ones. The exaggerated responses can move to a balanced level. Each new step and success needs to be reinforced, not so much by others, but by you. It's learning the phrase, "I can do this."

As you write, take the time to write a *future report on yourself in three years*. Describe what you really want to be like in three years. What will it take for you to arrive? At first you may not believe it's possible. That's all right. Rely on others' encouragement and belief in you.

Part of your story will be accessing your memories, both positive and negative. Memories can be a source of encouragement and benefit, or they may be detrimental and crippling. There are memories we wish we could retain and those we would like to eliminate. What's the best way to handle them?

The goal of the effective coping strategies is not to eliminate your traumatic memories. Unfortunately, the brain is not like the hard drive of your computer where you can simply delete a file; the memory is still there, but by using appropriate strategies, your response may ensure discomfort and growth rather than great upset and continued pain.

There is a unique type of memory that comes along with the unexpected event. Some call it "memory baggage." These memories are often intense and vivid. For some they are just pictures, but they could be full of color sights as well as smells and sounds. Some invoke the feeling of the senselessness of the event while others recur as a flashback or an intrusive thought. It's similar to a song getting stuck in your mind.

Many efforts to cope don't work; they are ineffective. Often when strategies to heal don't work, a person just tries harder, which leads to frustration.

These are the most common ineffective coping strategies:

- Attempting to think of something else as a substitute.
- Trying to think of something nice.
- Getting up and going into another room.
- Going to do some other activity.
- Talking to someone about any subject other than the incident itself.
- Drinking alcohol.
- Taking drugs.
- Trying to keep the memory from coming back. Holding it at arm's length.[9]

Here are some effective coping strategies:

1. Acknowledge the memory at a distance—admit to yourself that it exists and you can handle it.

2. Stop ruminating or constantly repeating the memory. Allow yourself two or three times to rehearse it mentally and then stop.

3. Dare to mention the event and call it or label it what it is. Talking about the event in as much detail as possible

will give you a sense of control. Find someone who is willing to listen to your narration.

4. Dictate the story to someone else or write the experience and its effects upon you as well as others.

5. Write out your story and its consequences in longhand.[10]

6. Read the story out loud. Rereading the story out loud with as much detail and feelings as you can muster can help you be in control. It's a way to take charge. You can't keep the memory from coming back, but you can make it your ally.

7. Another approach is dictating the story of the event into a recording device, again with as much detail as possible. It may take several tries to capture all of what occurred. Some have recorded a detailed narration and played it back several times a day. In doing so the impact of the event is lessened and in time the pain of going through this narration is lessened.

As one author said:

> It may be a struggle to express your experience, and the words may seem inadequate to begin with, but with practice you can better label your emotions. It is rather like giving a filename to a file on a computer: without such a label you are not able to access it properly or update its contents. You may feel that others will think you're mad if you tell them of your experience, but test this out with one or two people who are close to you. The alternative is that the thoughts, images and feelings travel interminably around well-worn grooves in your mind, making for poor company: you try to avoid them but keep bumping into them.[11]

Traumatic memories don't go away. Rituals are one way of controlling them. If you can put them in a safe place and then retrieve them on command they affect you less.

8. One approach that has worked well is inviting the memory in by saying, "Here you are again. I don't care for you. I don't like you. You've been disruptive and a real pain, but I can handle you. So, come on in and let's see what I can learn from you. In time you won't be that much a part of my life." I know this sounds strange, but it tends to be effective.

Memories pop up when you least want them. I've talked to many who would like a disappear switch. I've heard many say that their memories of the past haunt them. Many people feel their lives are haunted by thoughts and memories over which they have no control.

Some vacillate between a "get rid of the memory" agenda to a "just forget the past" mentality, and neither one of those approaches work.

Perhaps we need a book called *Peace with Our Memories*. I like what Robert D. Jones said about what is possible since our goal as believers is Christlikeness: "The good news is that if you belong to Jesus, God does have something better for you. God does not want to *remove* your memories; he wants to *redeem* them. He wants to *transform* them into something good, something that will make you more like Jesus."

The reality of a traumatic event is that it often eradicates the existence of positive, healing memories. Without them and other healing memories, we remain raw and broken.

Memories are not just random thoughts. They positively influence the present and future based on what we've experienced in the past.

Memories can be very helpful for our present and future, or they can hinder our present and future. Memories are storage containers.

One of the strongest aspects of human memory is the storage of *emotional* experiences. We remember emotions more than accurate facts. What about you?

There is another aspect to memory that could impact all of us—memory loss.

The loss of memory is one of our most important obstacles. Without memory we're limited. When our memory is severely impaired, we are no longer ourselves.

Memory is tied to our growth and recovery. There are some messages, however, that we wish would disappear. They are in our traumatic or unexpected memories. They float in and out of our minds automatically, and when they invade, they disrupt our lives.

There are many factors that impact your recovery process, and especially the severity of the original trauma. What is common to each and every healing process is the need to make peace with the memory of what has happened. This is vital. That tucked-away memory needs to be readily accessible so that the memory can inform the future rather than foreclose it. Too many today live with blockage of their memories.

How can you stabilize the symptoms of trauma? It requires a shift in understanding their meaning. The symptoms you experience need to be appreciated as life-preserving resources from a time of extraordinary circumstances. They serve a purpose. Healing begins not with trying to push the symptoms away but rather with trying to understand and befriend them for the great protection they have been. The symptoms reflect human resiliency and are not a sign of weakness or failure.

The memory of trauma, however, is not in the past. It is present and is reexperienced with the intensity of the original events. There is no time sequence—the memory simply is, without the perspective of sequence and understanding.

When trauma destroys belief in the future, there is no container for grief and so it remains unprocessed and grows in power. The fear of grief caused by events can foreclose the future as rapidly as the events themselves.

> We sometimes think of memory as the mind's safe-deposit box, a place where we deposit valuables in the form of remembered experiences. Just as we might head to the bank to open the locked metal container where we store our grandfather's solid-gold watch, so we might think that when we want to remember an event, we simply go to our brain's safe-deposit box to retrieve the event we want to examine. When we do, we assume it will be there, unchanged from when we last thought of it.

> But memory is in fact *not* like that locked metal box. Every time we remember something the memory itself changes, for the neural networks that are associated with that mental image are either reinforced to fire in a similar but slightly different fashion or they are shaped and altered to fire differently.[12]

Memories start with an experience, but we often "update" them based on images formed and shaped by the intensity of emotion. Details are altered, and some parts are reinforced and intensified while other parts are diminished. Keep these facts in mind as you gather your memories from your new experience. If you write them out and read them again and again, they'll become more balanced. (For more details and information on memories, see chapter 2 of my book *When the Past Won't Let You Go*.)

CHAPTER 9

Steps to Take to Regain Control—Emotions Included

W hen the unexpected occurs, it's easy to let its aftermath control our life. We have a choice between despair and hope. Despair can dominate our life and leave us wounded and a victim to whatever occurred. We learn to live our lives in fear. Or we can learn to live with hope and rebuild our lives with a new degree of safety. It's learning to live with our eyes on the past or the future. It's a choice between pessimism or optimism.

People who feel hopeful and optimistic increase their chances of bouncing back and may make things even better than before. Hope helps a person endure through difficult times, and optimism provides thoughts and images of things turning out well. Hope is what people have. Optimism is what people believe. Positive attitudes are usually linked to actions people can take, step by step, to get them from where they are to where they want to be. Coping is a choice and a process, different for each individual, in which a person keeps learning how to be better at handling difficult physical, mental, and emotional challenges.[1]

Our brain gives us the ability to recall memories of the past and imagine the future. We can remember good and bad things that have happened to us and can anticipate good and bad things that might happen.

A person full of hope (one who is hopeful) feels less despair. Hopeful people endure longer, which can lead to healing, rescue, or the end of bad circumstances. Hope allows people to imagine that their present difficult life will be better in the future. People who lack hope cannot imagine a better future for themselves. To be hopeless is discouraging.

Hope is meaningful when we are struggling to survive bad conditions.[2]

To let hope impact our life we need to be open to change.

From birth until death life contains multiple changes...even daily changes. Seasons of uncertainty, of change, as one stage winds down and a new one emerges. Any change—even those that are predictable and expected—carry elements of risk, insecurity, and vulnerability.

Stable times actually are the exception; change is the norm.

To some, the word *change* holds a sense of hope (there's that word again), connoting fresh possibilities or the potential for newness, and they embrace it accordingly. To others, even the word itself represents a threat, a disruption of comfort and safety, and they resist it as such.

When we resist change, we resist one or more of the three phases of its makeup. We may resist *letting go* of the old; we may resist the confusion of the in-between *neutral zone* state; or we may resist the uncertainties of making a risky new *beginning*. We resist it not because we can't accept the change but because we can't accept letting go of that piece of ourselves that we have to give up when or because the situation has changed.[3]

We can either just let change occur or we can be in charge of the changes in our life.

Below are some of the steps you can take to promote change. These will take time, effort, and a commitment to do something different. The following is what has worked for those who have moved forward in their lives:

1. Notice what stays the same every day.
2. Notice what is helpful each day. Write it down and be specific. Give as much detail as possible.
3. Notice what is different.
4. When change for the better takes place, note it, and figure out what was helpful about it.
5. Write a letter to yourself identifying what is working.

This assignment raises awareness of change by recognizing improvement, no matter how small that may be. In a family situation it may help to have the entire family undertake the assignment together, or have individual members complete the assignment separately and then share with others. The directions are, "You have acquired some expertise in managing your upset. Write a letter to yourself describing the steps you have taken and the skills and resources you have used to manage your upset." This is most effective when you read what you have written aloud.

Then there are some other intruders. They hit with the intensity of a tornado and the suddenness of an earthquake. They won't go away when you want them to, and there's no way to evict them. They're like a runaway train whose brakes have burned out. You feel totally out of control. Even though you may question the necessity of their presence, they do have a purpose. What do we call these "unfriendly" companions? *Emotions* or *feelings.*

During the upset you may experience a wide range of emotions, and perhaps some feelings you've never experienced before. It's not just the presence of the emotions that bother you; it's their intensity. Some of them may feel unbearable, even toxic.

The following are what to expect after an unexpected event:

- Fear of the trauma repeating. If someone you loved died, it can happen again to another person you love.

- Fear of the victim's similarity to you. If someone you know has been a victim of a crime, you can be too.

- Fear of aggressive loss of control. Anger can be a very scary thing, especially when you feel an inability to control yourself.

- Worry over the failure to prevent the event. You couldn't stop what happened and you are feeling ashamed and useless. The final section of this book will cover fear in detail.

- Rage at anyone you felt responsible for the fear. Everyone likes to blame someone, even if it's totally irrational.

- Rage at anyone lucky enough not to be involved. It's not fair what's happening to you. And then guilt over feeling such rage.

- Guilt over feeling that you were responsible. Somehow you are responsible for this event, even though you know you weren't.

- Guilt over surviving when others did not. Your joy at surviving while others did not survive is difficult to handle.

- Sadness over your painful loss. You are haunted with regrets.

People do recover from these events and find themselves happier and healthier than they ever were before. But you need to discover the symptoms that have weighed you down. Only then can you get rid of your pain, once and for all.[4]

When you understand that feeling an emotion is an unavoidable human condition and you know what to expect from emotions, you'll handle them better. Many believe they are alone in their experience of such intense feelings. They think, *No one else is like I am.* This misbelief keeps them from accepting their feelings, learning from them, and moving on to recovery. When trauma happens, there is an overload of emotions. And too often those emotions have no release and instead they are filed away and buried alive.

But what happens when intensely painful emotions brought on by trauma are stored intact in your nervous system for prolonged periods of time? These traumatic experiences will significantly color and shape your daily experiences until they are resolved. Merely talking or thinking about an emotionally painful experience will not always release the pain. Remember, our *intellect* cannot resolve what is *emotionally* imprinted.

During the emergency itself, something happens to most of us that allows us to set aside our feelings in order to deal with the urgent needs of the moment. We may experience a multitude of different feelings: fear, confusion, impotence, anguish, anxiety, frustration, anger, sadness. We also feel things you might not expect, like relief, closeness, silliness, pride in having helped, indifference, or numbness. The range of emotions is as varied as we are. None is right or wrong. Yet somehow we manage to hold these feelings in check until the immediate danger or incident has passed. That's what allows us to use our resources to be clear enough, calm enough, and in control to function.

Afterward, however, once the emergency has passed and your adrenaline has begun to retreat, those feelings may reemerge. It's not at all uncommon.

Feelings of helplessness or a lack of control on the scene of an emergency or a critical incident have been shown to increase pressure. It's entirely too common to hear comments such as, "I couldn't do anything," "I was powerless," or "It just all came down and I couldn't stop it." While this agony is familiar to anyone who wants to help people, those who are trained to save lives find it doubly difficult to tolerate that frustration.

More and more today we hear about survivor's guilt. Accidents, tornadoes, earthquakes, and terrorist attacks create a specific kind of remorse in those who survive the tragic event. There were many survivors of the Oklahoma City bombing with only minor injuries or no injuries at all. But many of them experienced survivor's guilt. The firemen and police officers who survived the collapse of the Twin Towers in New York talk about the sense of guilt in escaping death. There were those who didn't go to work that day or left early or went downstairs and missed the collapse of the towers. They too ask, "Why me?" but for different reasons. Even some of the family members of those who were lost in TWA Flight 800 ended up asking, "Why them? It should have been me. They were too young. I'm older."

This type of questioning often happens when the tragedy involves a child or someone you know well. The belief that it would have been more sensible for the tragedy to have happened to you rather than the other person is a clear indication of survivor's guilt. At the heart of these feelings could be the belief that you were allowed to avoid the tragedy at the cost of the other person. That feeling is rarely anchored in fact. Survivor's guilt is another form of self-blame. It's a way of saying, "If I had suffered more, you would have suffered less."

Helplessness brings with it a slew of other feelings, depending on your life experience and nature. Most people abhor the feeling of helplessness. Its residue is often anger, frustration, self-blame, or blame of others. In more serious reactions, a person can become obsessed by the experience and isolated.[5]

Rage and anger are trauma's offsprings. They often frighten the one experiencing the emotions as much as those on the receiving end.

For some who have been traumatized, the most accessible emotion at this time is anger. We use it to protect our hearts from experiencing pain and grief. This is why many will deny being angry, for to do so is to admit to the pain or grief or what created it. Consider these thoughts:

You could be angry at yourself for being alive and well while someone else isn't, or you could be angry about something you said or wished you had said or for not being yourself.

You could be angry because others don't understand. They don't get that you aren't going to get back to normal. And you're also angry because you're stuck in time while everyone else goes on living as if nothing had happened.

Hospital staff, doctors, paramedics, friends, relatives, and funeral directors may be on the receiving end of your anger.

> The power of anger after trauma is such that it feels like something destructive that will blow apart the mechanisms of coping and relationship. When properly appropriated, however, anger can be a productive energy that creates a new understanding of the world. Anger, like grief, must run its course along pathways and time periods that are not our choosing. Anger, however, cannot become healing or transformative if left on its own. It has to be respected and invited into consciousness before it will share its power. The real danger of anger is not the feeling itself, but the ways in which the attempt to contain it hollow out one's humanity rather than enhance it. Anger becomes destructive when it is used to diminish instead of serving as passion for change.[6]

One victim said:

> I finally realized that holding on to my anger kept me victimized. As much as I wanted someone to pay, I knew it wouldn't happen. So I decided on a 90-day plan. I would allow myself to keep 10 percent of my anger since I know I'm human and won't be perfect. But each day

for 90 days I would give up 1 percent of my anger. The fact that I had a goal and then developed a plan really encouraged my recovery. Each day I spent 15 to 20 minutes identifying who or what I wanted to avenge. I wrote it out each time and then put it in the form of a brief letter. I stood in a room and read it out loud unedited. Sometimes it wasn't pretty. And sometimes I read it to a friend because it helped having a live body there.

Each day I wrote the phrase, "I forgive you for…" and then put down the first reason I could think of for not forgiving. It was like I was full of rebuttals against forgiving. I would always end the morning by reading a praise psalm out loud. Then I would lift my hands to the Lord and give Him my anger for the day. Then I thanked Him for what He was doing, even if I didn't feel like it. I discovered many things through this. I was full of bitterness. It kept me pinned down and stuck. I didn't want to forgive. They didn't deserve it.

But I kept at it. I wondered after 30 days if I'd made even a 3 percent improvement. But by the time 60 days were over I felt ahead of schedule. I was improving, I was growing, I got well. Sometimes the anger and grief still hit me. I can live with that even if it's a companion the rest of my life. I have days and weeks when I feel whole again. Praise God for this.

AVOIDANCE OF EMOTIONS

Let's return to a topic talked about previously…emotions.

Most of us are understandably reluctant to address the distressful emotions that accompany grieving or trauma. After all, most choose to avoid pain if they can. Some avoidance can be helpful at times; for example, staying busy or steering clear of certain situations or topics are effective temporary means of emotion management. The problem occurs when the avoidance is used consistently to deny means of emotion management or when the avoidance is used consistently to deny legitimate feelings (e.g., blocking, minimizing, distracting, suppressing).

There are many reasons that a grieving person may avoid emotions. They may not believe that anything can be better if they experience and express them. This is often the case in the early phases of grief, when it's difficult to see that anything can ever be different, especially emotional pain. Some may fear that experiencing and expressing emotions will be a sign they're inadequate, weak, or disturbed. They may be concerned about their own reactions as well as the reactions of others. They may fear rejection or criticism from others because they judge some feelings as unacceptable. They may fear that experiencing and expressing their emotions will cause them to lose control. This is common for anyone grieving losses that are often beyond their control and in situations in which control was taken from them. They may lack awareness and experiencing skills.

It's important to explore the reasons you may avoid your emotions. Counselors often refer to this as "talking about the wall" rather than attempting to break down the wall. There are a number of questions to consider. Why avoid? What are you worried about? What if the emotions were approached? What is the worst and best that could happen? What helps? Is emotional avoidance tied only to the current upset or is this a consistent pattern? Where do the origins of reluctance to experience and express feelings come from?

Some refer to a few of their emotions as dark emotions. One of the helpful questions is, "How have my dark emotions made me strong?"

You can write or tell a story that details how the distressing emotions have made you stronger or transformed you in some way.

The focus here is not so much on provoking an emotional response as considering your emotions in light of what you've experienced. This strategy underscores the value of emotions and promotes acceptance of your emotional world.

We all have emotional legacies. This is why we see different responses to the unexpected. Often we can tell how a person will respond by knowing their experiences as a child. Those who were traumatized have probably not learned from their trauma, and it may limit a healthy response to overcoming the unexpected.

How do you respond to this event? So often the memories we have are tied into our emotions, or our emotions activate our memories. It can vary. I've talked to so many who said, "Memory! What memory? It's like someone took a butter knife and scraped all my memory cells off the brain! What's wrong with me?" We call this "normal." This is what happens when you experience what we call a traumatic event. I've explained this, but people will say, "But why? What's happened to me?" The answer is simple: When you experience trauma, the portion of your brain that is related to emotion and memory shrinks, and this can result in memory loss as well. The emergency alarm system often overreacts. If you can't remember anything, that's a normal response. There's a memory loss as well as time confusion. The brain can't put events in order, so the past might be seen as present and the present is seen as something from the past. No wonder there's confusion! Some sections in the brain that you want to work properly don't. The area of your brain that you want to be in charge such as the thinking could be shut down since emotions take over.

Remember, you want the thinking part of your brain in charge rather than the emotional. You don't want the brain under the influence of your emotions. Often those under this influence begin to become negative.[7]

One of the most frequent symptoms I find in those who have been through trauma is sleep disturbance, either not sleeping or restless sleeping in which you wake up in the morning totally not rested. Your body is reflecting the conflict that is going on in your brain.

These are steps to take to assist you in sleeping.

If you are struggling with anxiety, sleep will be a challenge. If your mind won't shut off and continues to work, you can interrupt this busyness. What we take into our thought life and mind can either help you or have a detrimental effect. Time after time, as I've sat with those after their unexpected experience, I've heard this struggle. In most cases it's not just the event but a pattern of doing things that will hinder sleep.

The following list of scriptures and prayers have helped to calm many and activate the thinking part of their brain. Sit on the side of the bed and read the scriptures and prayer out loud and then turn off the lights. You may need to do this more than once. You are taking the Word of God into the thinking part of your brain in a visual and auditory way.

> When you lie down, you will not be afraid;
> When you lie down, your sleep will be sweet.
> Do not be afraid of sudden fear
> Nor of the storm of the wicked when it comes [since
>   you will be blameless];
> For the Lord will be your confidence, firm *and* strong,
> And will keep your foot from being caught [in a trap]
>   (Proverbs 3:24-26 AMP).

> I lie down and sleep,
> and all night long the Lord protects me (Psalm 3:5 GNT).

> If I'm sleepless at midnight,
> I spend the hours in grateful reflection (Psalm 63:6 MSG).

> When my anxious thoughts multiply within me,
> Your consolations delight my soul (Psalm 94:19 NASB).

In peace I will lie down and sleep in peace,
for you alone, Lord,
make me dwell in safety (Psalm 4:8).

In a dream, a vision of the night,
When sound sleep falls on men...
Then He opens the ears of men,
And seals their instruction (Job 33:15-16 nasb).

Dear God,

We give thanks for the darkness of the night where lies the world of dreams. Guide us closer to our dreams so that we may be nourished by them. Give us good dreams and memory of them so that we may carry their poetry and mystery into our daily lives

Grant us deep and restful sleep that we may wake refreshed with strength enough to renew a world grown tired.

We give thanks for the inspiration of stars, the dignity of the moon, and the lullabies of crickets and frogs.

Let us restore the night and reclaim it as a sanctuary of peace, where silence shall be music to our hearts and darkness shall throw light upon our souls. Good night. Sweet dreams. Amen.

Michael Leuing, *A Common Prayer*

Continue to read the scriptures and prayer each night before bed and spend a few minutes praying for peaceful sleep. Each morning reflect on changes in your sleep patterns and the progress you are making in sleeping through the night.

Let's consider something different—what I call exception questions. These are used to discover times when you are deliberately or spontaneously *handling* difficulties, even to a small degree. These questions reveal ways in which you can be in control of your problems rather than your problems controlling you (e.g., managing the upset rather than the upset controlling you).

- What are the times when your upset seems more manageable?

- What are the times when you feel you are more a survivor and less a victim of what occurred?

- Tell me about the moments when you forget you're grieving or upset.

- When you have a better day, what is different in terms of managing all of this?

Too often we ask ourselves, "Why…?" when this question can't be answered.

But what happens when the question is changed from "Why?" to "How?" "How am I making myself depressed?" "How am I making myself so worried?" "How am I making myself so upset?" "How am I making myself so angry?" "How am I creating my anxiety?" "How am I making myself feel so far away from God?" Awareness comes when questions are asked in this fashion.

A very simple approach and one that works well with those unable to recapture some of their specific thoughts is to count their thoughts as they occur. This assists in several ways. It helps you feel as though you're gaining some control over your situation, it helps you recognize how automatic your thoughts are, and it helps give you a better perspective on your thinking. This is a beginning step in recognizing how your thoughts affect emotions and behavior.

The feeling or sense of safety is vital for survival. It's a must. When this is ripped away from us, as it is with the unexpected, our lives become chaotic. It takes time, creativity, and patience to rebuild our security.

One of the ways of beginning to restore this sense of safety is in your mind or imagination. Whenever you begin to feel overwhelmed or unsafe, the following is something you can do. Your imagination is both a gift and a powerful tool that can stabilize your life.

Select a picture or image that is calming and gives you a sense of safety. You choose what works for you.

Focus on the image. Some write it out or draw it out. Where is it in your body? What are the feelings you're experiencing now? What is helping you feel safe at this time?

Now intensify your image of safety. What about this gives you a sense of safety? It could be something from your past that's real or something you create. What one word describes this safe place? Describe your feelings when you are in this safe place. How often do you want to bring your safe image into your imagination? If your body could talk to you when you bring this up, what would it say to you?

Some have found it helpful to practice this several times a day until your sense of safety is stronger. Don't let what happened take this away from you.

Here is a variation of creating a place or sense of safety. This is something to be used during a time of crisis or trauma or when you're feeling unsafe.

Walk about 100 yards, and as you do this, recall all the bad that has happened until you reach the end of your 100 yards. Then turn around, and as you head back, think about all the good that has happened and envision being safe. Repeat this multiple times until the good is in charge in your mind and you're feeling safe. Many who have done this have found it to be very helpful.

Imagery is actually the basis for our thought processes and is a way to process information. The words we first develop as an infant probably occur because we first had images in our mind.

Imaging is the forming of mental pictures or images. We have a tendency to ultimately become like that which we imagine or image ourselves as being. If we image ourselves as failing, we are more likely to fail. If we imagine ourselves as succeeding in some task, there is a greater likelihood that we will succeed. Images that we hold on to and reinforce eventually seep into the unconscious part of our minds.

Imaging can dramatically change our emotional state. It can counter our self-defeating behaviors and negative self-talk, and promote healing from trauma.

We can image particular scenes such as a walk through the woods or along a riverbank or by the seashore—any peaceful, quiet experience. This is one way to induce peaceful, restful feelings when we are anxious or apprehensive.

People who image under these circumstances can recapture the peaceful emotions they have experienced at some time in their life. The associations made unconsciously in their brain of such literal walks with the accompanying feelings of restfulness and peace are reawakened in the imaging experiencing.

The Psalms and the parables of Jesus provide a rich collection of descriptive life experiences for imaging. Jesus used imagery abundantly in His earthly ministry. An intimate relationship with Jesus generates a host of powerful experiences that become a part of the fabric of our mind. Resurrecting these experiences by imaging will vaporize any threatening cloud.[8]

One person I worked with shared that making mistakes created three different emotional responses for them: anxiety, depression, and anger. And this tended to happen more than once each day. The procedure to follow in such cases is close your eyes and begin to imagine such a situation happening. Experience it and see it as clearly as possible. Now "see" the colors and shapes, "hear" the sounds, and notice as many details as possible. Picture yourself making several of your negative and self-defeating statements to yourself. Picture the situation until you begin to feel the negative emotion. When you do, raise your hand. Begin imagining the worst possible consequences of your unhealthy thoughts. One individual said, "If I continue to believe that mistakes are so awful, I'll freeze up every time. I won't be able to function at work. I could lose my job. Friends will turn me off. And the more uptight I get, the worse it will be." Now what is the result of this?

Imagery can help identify your thoughts and the relationship of thoughts to feelings, behavior, and consequences. By using role visualization, relive a recent unpleasant situation and specify the thoughts, feelings, and actions that occur as the situation is relived. After you learn how to do this, you can recreate several past situations. Describe each situation as though it were happening right now.

Image as vividly as you can, and describe the details of a situation in which you became upset in the past or you might become upset in the future. Perhaps it's making a mistake, or your spouse mistreating you, someone taking you for granted, or not performing as well as you feel you should. As you visualize this situation, let yourself feel your emotional response, whether it be anger, depression, fear, etc. Get in touch with this upsetting feeling as much as possible. (Take 10 to 20 seconds to do this.) Now force yourself to change this feeling to one of disappointment, regret, annoyance, or irritation, so that you feel displeased but not upset. (Again allow 10 to 20 seconds.) Now do it again so you feel neutral.

Another imagery exercise is called visual motor behavioral rehearsal (VMBR). It is usually used to help a person perform some type of behavior that was previously avoided because of fear. Select a quiet place at home, engage in some relaxation exercises, and then imagine performing the desired behavior—but on a gradual basis. (Relaxation exercises are for the purpose of relieving tension from the muscles and helping eliminate stress.)

Focus upon your thought life. Imagery clarifies problems because it can. The distortion of reality in the counselee's image can offer a clue as to the reason for inappropriate reaction. It may be helpful to

ask some of the following questions in order to discover the images
that are accompanying your thinking.

"Do you see a picture as you're talking?"

"Would you please describe it?"

"Is it in color?"

"Is there sound?"

"Are you moving?"

"Is anyone else moving?"

"Do you smell anything?"

"Do you feel anything?"

Thought stopping is a helpful procedure to assist with many of
the thoughts that seem out of control, especially those that keep us
unsafe.

Thought stopping involves concentrating on the unwanted
thoughts and, after a short time, suddenly stopping and emptying
one's mind. The command "Stop!" or a loud noise is generally used
to interrupt the unpleasant thoughts.

Thought stopping is an assertive response and needs to be followed by positive thoughts substitutions, that is, reassuring, realis-
tic, positive, or self-accepting statements.

It's been well established that negative and frightening thoughts
invariably create negative and frightening emotions. If thoughts can
be controlled, the overall stress level can be significantly reduced.
For this to be effective, thought stopping must be practiced consciously throughout the day for several weeks with consistency.

The first step is to explore and list the stressful or upsetting
thoughts. What are the results of your trauma?

The second step of thought stopping involves thought substitu-
tion. It helps to write out as many new thoughts as possible. In place
of obsessive, negative thoughts, create some positive, assertive statements that are appropriate in this situation.

When you think, imagine, daydream, or fantasize, you often
give yourself a set of instructions that ensures your acting in a fearful

manner or responding as if the upsetting event is still present. These instructions soon become habits. One of the best ways to break a habit is by setting up a more powerful counter habit. Here the counter habit you're trying to achieve is that of teaching yourself not to experience the negative or painful thoughts. With "thought switching," you don't try to stop or eliminate your worrisome thoughts of doom as directly as you do with thought stoppage. Instead, you (1) select a series of counter thoughts and (2) deliberately strengthen these new thoughts until they become strong enough to override or replace the negative thoughts.[9] This is especially effective with fear. The purpose is to replace any fear self-instructions with positive self-instructions.

Step One: The first step is to recall what you usually say prior to the fear on which you are now working. List the self-instructions you give yourself (the small, detailed ones as well as the big, overwhelming self-instructions).

Step Two: For each of these self-instructions, set up a list of coping self-instructions. Your aim is to set up the opposite habit of thinking so that you'll be able to handle whatever happens.

Step Three: Put each of the new self-instructions you have worked out for yourself on a separate card. The order doesn't matter. Carry the cards with you or stick them in a convenient place—in your purse, on top of the night table, by the telephone, in your computer bag, etc.

Step Four: Take a group of actions you perform fairly frequently every day: drinking coffee or soda, changing channels on the TV set, running a comb through your hair, washing your hands, making a phone call. Say the new instruction before you carry out an action.

If you fail in your first attempt at stopping a thought, it may mean that you've selected one that's very difficult to eliminate.

Writing down thoughts and ideas helps to get them out of your memory where they will otherwise be kept alive by the memory-refreshing mechanisms of your brain. Your notebook, therefore, serves as an external memory. It can be taken with you everywhere. See it as an extension of your brain.

Perhaps the best way to deal with emotions that invade your life is to follow the example of a hiker who had just read the Forest Service instructions of what to do when encountering wild animals, especially mountain lions. This man was jogging with his dog and came upon a mountain lion. The lion began to stalk the man and then ran after him. Fortunately, the man remembered what he had read. He stopped, turned around, and faced the mountain lion. The lion wasn't expecting this, so it stopped and walked away. Your emotions are like that mountain lion. Face them head-on, listen to their message, and eventually you'll rise above them. And one way to do this is to write about them.

Remember, you have more control over these emotions than you realize, whether it be fear, anger, sadness, anxiety, guilt, or depression. It's possible to welcome them into your life, talk with them, learn from them, and even in the moment lower their intensity. Using one of God's gifts—our imagination—see in your mind a volume dial like you would find on a radio. This is like a "feelings" dial. It has numbers on it from one to ten, from low to the most intense. Look carefully at this dial in your mind. See what it's made of. Imagine how it feels in your hand. Now select the unpleasant feeling and determine what number on your dial reflects how weak or strong it is. What number is the dial on now? What is it like to be on that number? What would it be like to be on two? On eight? Or somewhere in the middle? If you would like to turn it down, what number would you turn it to? Now turn the dial lower and lower until it goes down one number from where you started. Keep turning it down lower and lower and lower. Do it slowly until you find the intensity you want. Go slow and breathe deeply. What is it like when you reach the desired number?

Yes, there is a lot of material in this chapter. It may help to reread this and be sure to complete the suggestions. They can make a difference.

CHAPTER 10

You, Your Family, and Survival

It may seem as though your unthinkable event has damaged you or your family beyond all hope of repair. For a while it feels that way. As deep as the damage goes, however, you can survive, and so can your family.

Survival is a choice. Like so many other issues in life, we do have a choice regarding how to respond to the curveballs thrown at us.

If you think that things will never be the same, you may be right. They probably won't be. These events will create change. Our response to them makes the difference. The question is, do you want to be a victim of the direction this change takes you, or do you want to be in charge of it? Everyone has a choice after a major unexpected event hits. It's true that it seems like it takes forever to move on. The definition of a survivor is a person (or family) who gets knocked down and stays down for the count…then gets back up and does things differently. The non-survivor just gets back in the ring and gets hit all over again. That hurts! And when you're dealing with a lingering or ongoing issue, there's enough pain already.

If you've already experienced any of these unexpected events, you know what I'm saying. Some families draw closer together, and some become more compassionate. Some individuals stagnate while others grow, even as they carry wounds and scars. I've sat with all of them.

Many families, instead of working out solutions for their pain and problems together, begin to attack each other. If conflicts have been buried for years, the unexpected lifts the restraints, and issues erupt with a new source of fuel. Any buried problems of the past will find themselves coming to the surface and influencing the current situation. Now your family has to deal not only with the current event but with other unresolved issues as well. Each drains energy needed to cope with the other.

A family works together like a large body. Each person is an integral part of their body. If anyone refuses to cooperate with others and does his or her own thing, all the other parts or people are affected. They have to learn to adjust. Sometimes they must assume new roles. And sometimes they remained fractured. I've seen a number who stay stagnated for years. It's not a pretty sight.

It's similar to balancing an old-fashioned scale. If something is added to one side, it alters the other side by the same amount, but in the opposite direction. If the scale is ever to be balanced again, something has to be added or subtracted to both sides.

Families are like that scale. The members have to adjust to the change and get back into balance. Many aspects of family life—including power, responsibilities, and roles—may need to be reassigned. The longer the central individual impacted has been in the family or the greater the significance or their position, the more adjustments need to be made

I've seen cases in which a child committed serious offenses that drew attention away from a couple's marriage problems. When this person was no longer at home, marital problems became apparent, and some other person became the troublemaker to ease the marital tensions. It works the other way as well. Perhaps the marital problems could be swept under the carpet as long as all was smooth sailing with the children. But when the upset arose, it drew out all the tension that had been fostering between the couple.

Between the time an upset occurs and the individual family members discover their new roles and begin to stabilize, there's a time of uncertainty and turmoil. This usually feels uncomfortable. It's difficult to make some of the necessary changes. Each family member needs time and space to deal with this issue in his or her own way. It may take a while for each one to find a new role. Each feels like a juggler at times, trying to deal with his or her own needs and still be helpful to other family members. I've seen both types of families—those who were supportive and those who blamed.

After an event hits, you'll also have to weigh the needs of particular family members against the needs of the whole family. You'll have to work to achieve a balance. And it's not always easy.

What is your approach to survive a crisis? How do entire families survive, or anyone for that matter? How will you survive? Must a person have a certain type of background or upbringing to be a survivor when a family is impacted? No. With the right approach, anyone can survive the experience. Surviving is different from resolving or growing.

I never expected to have my only son born profoundly mentally retarded because of unexpected brain damage and then suddenly die at the age of 22. But it happened.

Over the years, my wife and I have learned the truth and significance of many passages from God's Word. One passage in particular came alive as we depended on it more and more: "Consider it all joy, my brethren, when you encounter various trials, knowing that the testing [or trying] of your faith produces endurance" (James 1:2-3 NASB).

The Amplified Version goes on to say, "And let endurance have its perfect result and do a thorough work, so that you may be perfect and completely developed [in your faith], lacking in nothing" (verse 4).

Learning to put that attitude into practice is a process and is not always easy. The passage does not say "respond this way immediately." You have to feel the pain and grief first, and then you'll be able to consider "it all joy."

What does the word *consider* mean? As I studied in commentaries, I discovered that it refers to an internal attitude of the heart or mind that allows the trials and circumstances of life to affect us either adversely or beneficially. Another way James 1:2 might be translated is this: "Make up your mind to regard adversity as something to welcome or be glad about."

The words "make up your mind" are critical. You have the power to decide what your attitude will be. You can say about a trial, "That's terrible. It's totally upsetting. That's the last thing I wanted for my life. Why did it have to happen now? Why me?" And rant and rave!

The other way of "considering" the same difficulty is to say, "It's not what I wanted or expected, but it's here. There are going to be some difficult times, but how can I make the best of them?" Don't ever deny the pain or hurt you might have to go through, but always ask, "What can I learn from it? How can I grow through this? How can I use it for God's glory?" It may take you months to get to this place. That's normal.

The verb tense used in the word *consider* indicates a decisiveness of action. It's not an attitude of resignation: "Well, I'll just give up. I'm stuck with this problem that's the way life is." If you resign yourself, you will sit back and do nothing. But James 1:2 indicates you will have to *go against* your natural inclination to see the trial as a negative.

Attitude doesn't just happen—it's cultivated.

Attitude doesn't just happen—it's learned.

Attitude doesn't just happen—it's desired.

Attitude doesn't just happen—it's practical.

Attitude doesn't just happen—it's a choice.

Attitude doesn't just happen—it's practiced just as is resilience.

When the unthinkable happens, you can tell yourself that something is bad, it's destructive, it's negative, or you can say, "I can learn through this, and as bad as it is, there will be meaning."

There will be some moments when you'll have to remind yourself, "I think there's a better way of responding to this. Lord, I really want You to help me see it from a different perspective." Then your mind will shift to a more constructive response. This often takes a lot of work on your part. Discovering the truth of the verses in James and many other passages like those will enable you to develop a biblical perspective on life. And that is the ultimate survival tool.

Remember, God created us with both the capacity and the freedom to determine how we respond to the unexpected incidents life brings our way. You wish that a certain event had never occurred, but you can't change the fact that it did. The key word here is *attitude*. Listen to the story of one woman and impact of attitude:

> The day had started out rotten. I overslept and was late for work. Everything that happened at the office contributed to my nervous frenzy. By the time I reached the bus stop for my homeward trip, my stomach was one big knot.
>
> As usual, the bus was late, and jammed. I had to stand in the aisle. As the lurching vehicle pulled me in all directions, my gloom deepened.
>
> Then I heard a deep voice from up front boom, "Beautiful day, isn't it?" because of the crowd I could not see that man, but I could hear him as he continued to comment on the spring scenery, calling attention to

each approaching landmark. This church. That park. This cemetery. That firehouse. Soon all the passengers were gazing out the windows. The man's enthusiasm was so contagious I found myself smiling for the first time that day.

We reached my stop. Maneuvering toward the door, I got a look at our "guide": a plump figure with a black beard, wearing dark glasses and carrying a thin white cane. Incredible! He was blind.

I stepped off the bus and, suddenly, all my built-up tension drained away. God in His wisdom had sent a blind man to help me see—to see that though there are times when things go wrong, when all seems dark and dreary, it is still a beautiful world. Humming a tune, I raced up the steps to my apartment. I couldn't wait to greet my husband with, "Beautiful day, isn't it?"

Those who survive realize that God is in control of the way things turn out. We do all that we can do, but then we rest in Him. As it says in Psalm 37:

> Do not fret because of those who are evil
>   or be envious of those who do wrong:
> for like the grass they will soon wither,
>   like green plants they will soon die away.
> Trust in the LORD and do good:
>   dwell in the land and enjoy safe pasture.
> Take delight in the LORD
>   and he will give you the desires of your heart.
> Commit your way to the LORD;
>   trust in him and he will do this:
> He will make your righteous reward shine like the dawn,
>   your vindication like the noonday sun.

Be still before the LORD
   and wait patiently for him;
do not fret when people succeed in their evil ways,
   when they carry out their wicked schemes.
Refrain from anger and turn from wrath;
   do not fret—it leads only to evil (verses 1-8).

In order to survive, you learn to express your feelings—all of them—which means you need a feeling vocabulary. Survivors find healthy ways to express hurt, anger, bitterness, depression, and resentment. They don't bottle up the feelings, nor do they merely complain. They talk, they write, they share, they pray, and they cry—men and women alike. Bottled-up feelings fester and remain alive and interfere with life.

You'll be angry. Oh, will you ever! But that's okay. It's a feeling that mobilizes you into action. Anger is a sign of protest. It's a natural and predictable emotion after a crisis or loss. It's a reaction against something that shouldn't have happened. It's a way of fighting back when you feel helpless. Your perception of the way things are or the way they should be has been altered. Your belief system has been damaged. Anger is a normal reaction when you are deprived of something you value.

Too often, there is no appropriate object upon which to vent our anger, so we begin looking for anything! At whom do we get angry most often? God. We blame Him—He shouldn't have done this or He shouldn't have allowed that. He's supposed to do things right, which means according to the way we want it! Why didn't He protect or redirect us or our loved one, especially when we prayed every day? Whom do we blame?

When you blame God, it can be unnerving and unsettling to other people. They either respond with Christian clichés, or they try to convince you that your anger at God is irrational. They fail to realize that nothing they say will help, because you are living on emotions at this point. Even though you may be raising questions, you're not really looking for answers.

We also get angry at others who haven't had to experience what we've gone through. Because they haven't experienced—or we think they haven't experienced—the devastation that we have, part of us wants them to have the opportunity.

You may get angry at those who fail to reach out and support you during this time of trouble. When we hurt, we want to be acknowledged. We don't want people to pretend that everything is okay, because it isn't. And in some cases, it will never be—at least not in the way we have always defined *okay*. Of course, part of the reason we end up feeling isolated is that few people have been taught how to minister to people during a time of need. Fortunately, this is starting to change.

You must learn to use anger's energy to do something constructive.

Perhaps you could write a letter (don't mail it!) to whomever you're angry at, and then sit in a room and read it aloud. Many people have found release by journaling each day. The point is, those who are resilient come to grips with their anger, and their other feelings, in constructive ways.

A friend of mine, Jessica Shaver, wrote the following poem that depicts what so many people have discovered.

I Told God I Was Angry

I told God I was angry.
I thought He'd be surprised.
I thought I'd kept hostility
quite cleverly disguised.

I told the Lord I hate Him.
I told Him that I hurt.
I told Him that He isn't fair.
I told God I was angry
but I'm the one surprised.

"What I've known all along,"
He said, "you've finally realized.
At last you have admitted
What's really in your heart.
Dishonesty, not anger,
was keeping us apart.

Even when you hate Me
I don't stop loving you.
Before you can receive that love
you must confess what's true.
In telling Me the anger
you genuinely feel,
it loses power over you
permitting you to heal."
I told God I was sorry
and He's forgiven me.
The truth that I was angry
has finally set me free.

Over the years, we've found that families who have difficulty coping with the unexpected frequently hurt one another by keeping silent. Silence can destroy. It causes us to speculate about what others are thinking and feeling. During a crisis, interaction among family members is vital. Others, however, retreat into their own inner worlds and don't express their thoughts or feelings. Sometimes certain family members want to talk, but others don't. Family members may not communicate during difficult times because they never learned to talk when everything was going well. People aren't likely to have the energy, time, and capability to learn communication skills when life is falling apart around them.

What happens when you ask a family member, whether an adult, an adolescent, or a child, "What's going on with you?" or "What are you thinking or feeling?" Often you hear, "I don't know," or "Nothing." Help others out by providing them with a vocabulary. Time and time again I've seen the change in the interaction when this is done. There are numerous ways this can be accomplished, but for years I've used the Ball of Grief (which I have provided below). There are many ways to use this. Have multiple copies available, and either have set times to use it or use it when you need interaction. You could call it Ball of Grief Time and set an amount of time such as Ball of Grief Drill—two minutes or five minutes or whatever you feel is needed. Everyone has a copy of the Ball of Grief and a highlighter. When the time begins, they color in whatever they're experiencing, and at the end of the time everyone stops and shares what they've colored. Questions to ask during this time are "What's another word for that?" or "What do you want to do with that emotion?" or "How could you express that?" The list of questions is endless, and some discussions can continue for extended periods of time. You may be surprised at the results.

GRIEF...
A Tangled "Ball" of Emotions

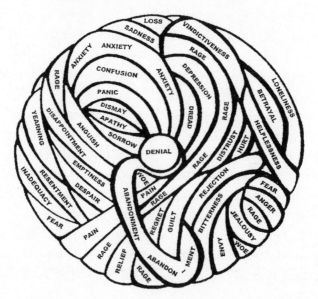

Most people don't realize that a silent person has power over other family members. For those who want to talk, silence adds to the pressure of the crisis, and they end up feeling rejected and isolated. Survivors learn to draw on their own strengths and gifts and use them effectively, yet they still ask for and can accept assistance from others. They can also express concern and warmth to others. Silence is a characteristic of dysfunctional families; it destroys and deadens hope. And as the silence progresses, estrangement and frustration increase. If you don't know what to say, begin with a statement such as "I wish I knew what to say, but I don't." It's a contribution. Don't allow one person's silence to isolate the rest of you.

Those who survive and grow concentrate more on solutions than on blame. Blame is one of the most significant characteristics of individuals and families who *don't* make it during difficult times. No one likes being out of control and left hanging. We yearn for some closure, to discover what created the problem in the first place. If we have an explanation for that horrific unexpected event, we can understand it better, handle it better, and feel relieved that someone else was at fault. The more serious it was, the greater the need we feel to discover the cause. Statements that start with the words, "If only you had/hadn't…" or "Why didn't you/Why did you…" begin to fly between one person and another. If a family member knows the other person's areas of vulnerability, accusations can get vicious.

You may not want to blame others, but blame directs the attention away from you. You know it doesn't make sense, but good sense doesn't often prevail after a crisis. Rather, the struggle for a reason for the difficulty becomes uppermost. When you blame, you create a war zone and the other side retaliates.

Because everyone is vulnerable at this time, accusations and other comments penetrate deep into the mind and heart of the one on the receiving end. They'll be remembered for years. No one wants to be unfairly accused or blamed.

In the book of Proverbs, we read, "There are those who speak rashly like the thrusts of a sword" (12:18 AMP), and "When there are many words, transgression and offense are unavoidable" (10:19 AMP). These verses clearly reflect the pain of unfair accusation.

It's a difficult temptation to resist. But blaming only makes the problem worse.

Blame is so common. We can put this on ourselves, which usually leads to survivor guilt, as in the case of some of our disasters. We think we could have or should have done more. Most of the time our response is to blame others and shift the responsibility elsewhere regardless of the facts. It's also saying that outside of me is in control. Blaming others also says, "I wasn't in control as I should have been."

Families who do not cope well often magnify the seriousness of their problems. They take it to the extreme and imagine the worst possible consequences instead of being hopeful or waiting to see what the actual results will be. They interact too much and in the wrong direction. When they discuss their crises only among themselves without outside objective assistance, they easily become pessimistic. They're not solution-oriented but problem-centered. They often use the "victim phrases" that reflect a desire to just give up:

"I can't…"

"That's a problem."

"I'll never…"

"That's awful!"

"Why is life this way?"

"If only…"

"Life is a big struggle."

"What will I do?"

These kinds of statements take a problem from bad to worse. And sometimes they can be self-fulfilling prophecies. Rose-colored glasses may not be helpful, but magnifying glasses can be just as detrimental.

Bitterness will try to creep in, but survivors shut the door in its face. They refuse to live in the past or permit a situation to stop them in their tracks with no hope for the future. Bitterness comes from focusing on the unfairness of whatever has happened. It's like a war-plane's radar locking onto a target. Bitterness leads to resentment, and the bitter person becomes a victim.

Sometimes in discussing a painful situation, you hear someone say, "Don't tell me to forgive! I'm not about to. They don't deserve it."

One may need to take action, such as reading books about the problem. Another may get more comfort from prayer and quiet walks; another may need to put it out of his mind, occupying his time and thoughts with anything but the problem. The families who cope most successfully with a crisis are those who respect each other's personality differences. If a person needs to talk or do some-thing—or needs privacy and quiet—that's all right. It helps to ask, "What can I do for you?" or "How can I help the most?"

Maybe your family is not in a healthy place. That's all right. But they are good goals to work on—ones that will not only help you cope with this crisis, but will make you and your family stronger and better afterward as well.

I asked others to share things they did that helped them survive their experience. Perhaps their answers will help you as well:

- "I turned to the Lord, spouse, godly friends, and profes-sionals for counsel. For some time it really did feel like mere survival. The pain was so great and the grieving so deep there were days I did not function well…Coming to the place where I could even believe all that happened took time."

- "I went on with my life with a new realization: I was a godly servant only to find out that I was an ungodly, codependent doormat. With this realization came action in the areas of counseling, reading, and Christian group help to start anew."

- "The first thing we did was call some very close friends—at 2 a.m.—and cried and prayed with them. We then shared it through some tears with our Sunday School class, who was very supportive and still is. I felt we needed to have others praying, and I didn't think keeping it quiet would allow for the body of Christ to apply prayer—it would only be those whom we told. So we had to get it out. It also opened doors for others to tell us that they, too, were living with the same thing. In some cases they didn't tell others, and in other cases they had talked freely about it."

- "I went on with my life by staying as busy as I could. I rearranged furniture and the bedrooms in the house— we bought a new couch and even a new car to replace what we lost."

- "We made sure we had time to get away together and talk. We had 'dates' at least once a week. Thanks to the availability of my parents, we were able to get away for occasional weekends and one time for a one-week cruise. Sometimes we used the time 'away' to listen to one another's pain and work on the next move and other times we would agree to 'have fun' and not mention one things about our situation. Sometimes we needed to get away from it all and remember our love and com-mitment for one another. During one of those getaways (Valentine's) we went to the same hotel where we spent our honeymoon (even the same room). Then we made a list of ten things we appreciated about one another. It was healing and affirming during a time when we other-wise felt unloved and unvalued."

- "I began a journal where I wrote one thing I was thankful for each day."
- "I read the Psalms and Job in *The Message*."
- "I sought out an older Christian woman and met weekly for prayer and mentoring."

These ideas may help you, or you may find other things more helpful. But whatever you do, find something that works. You can survive. Life can be good again, but it's up to you to make it happen.

CHAPTER 11

Biblical View of Suffering

There are times when our best defenses are totally inadequate, when all the tricks and strategies we have learned simply are not enough and we feel powerless, with seemingly no recourse but to rail against the unfairness of life and to wish for better times.

If wishes were reality, everything would go as we want. There would be no upsets, no downswings, and no fears or anxieties to interrupt our story. Like characters in a fairy tale, we would whisk away our hardships by rubbing a magic lamp or wishing on the first evening star.

The idea of "happily ever after" might be the stuff of make-believe, but its underlying desire is very real and very resilient. Whether we use yesterday's magic or today's power of positive thinking, we still want a direct line to health, happiness, and success in our everyday lives.

The fact is that sometimes we can't have what we want. Real life is a constantly changing road—some of it predictable, some of it totally out of control. We certainly help things along by eating right and living right. We can't prevent a major flood or the death of a loved one. Despite our best intentions, we may still get fired from our job. With or without our consent, sunny skies can become stormy, the stock market can go haywire, and the kindest people can come to harm.

When things change suddenly, they can shake up our world, sometimes with painful results that come back to destroy our emotional equilibrium long after the traumatic events themselves have passed.

"It isn't fair."

"I'm in shock. I never expected to win!"

"I don't believe this is happening to me."[1]

I wish we could avoid suffering and just sail through life without it. With many unthinkable events it's a companion. We see suffering, however, as being the exception in life. But have you considered that suffering may be the norm and suffering-free times are exceptions? For most of us, this thought is a major source of discomfort. Perhaps the best way to think about this is to look at the Scriptures for clarification.

The Word of God actually teaches the *certainty of suffering*. We all suffer. We don't want to, but we do.

All Christians are sure to suffer. In this world, you and I will suffer. The Scriptures are quite blunt:

> Dear friends, do not be surprised at the fiery ordeal that has come on you to test you, as though something strange were happening to you (1 Peter 4:12).

> Jesus said, "In this world you will have trouble" (John 16:33).

These passages are quite direct. They don't say "it may" or "it might be possible," but it is definite you "will"!

Not only is it certain, it's a certainty.

CALLING TO SUFFER

In the Bible there seems to be a call to suffer, which chafes against today's Christian culture, where many times there is a call to comfort.

> For it has been granted to you on behalf of Christ not only to believe in him, but also to suffer for him (Philippians 1:29).

> In fact, everyone who wants to live a godly life in Christ Jesus will be persecuted (2 Timothy 3:12).

> Consider it pure joy, my brothers and sisters, whenever you face trials of many kinds (James 1:2).

> If you are insulted because of the name of Christ, you are blessed, for the Spirit of glory and of God rests on you (1 Peter 4:14).

Did you catch the words that go along with suffering? It's been granted to you as though it's not just a reality but a privilege. It goes along with a godly life, and it's a way to express joy.

So, what is the *purpose of suffering*?

Many can handle almost any amount of evil and suffering if they believe it is for a purpose. The Bible helps us understand that there is no such thing as meaningless suffering and describes its many purposes. Consider the following purposes:

- So that we will rely not upon ourselves but upon God (see 2 Corinthians 1:9).

- So that we may become more sensitive to others and so that we can comfort them with the comfort we ourselves have received (see 2 Corinthians 1:4; Luke 22:31-33).

- So that through our sufferings, the saving grace of God will reach more and more people (see 2 Corinthians 4:15).

- So that God may receive praise (see 1 Peter 1:6-7).
- So that our character may be developed (see Romans 5:3-5).

Paul, the apostle, is a model for us in many ways. He said,

> I am not saying this because I am in need, for I have learned to be content whatever the circumstances. I know what it is to be in need, and I know what it is to have plenty. I have learned the secret of being content in any and every situation, whether well fed or hungry, whether living in plenty or in want (Philippians 4:11-12).

> Brothers and sisters, I do not consider myself yet to have taken hold of it. But one thing I do: Forgetting what is behind and straining toward what is ahead, I press on toward the goal to win the prize for which God has called me heavenward in Christ Jesus (Philippians 3:13-14).

Pressing on regardless of circumstances had nothing to do with Paul's personality but was a part of his character, learned over time through his relationship with Christ. This is great news because the belief that people are resilient by nature is simply not true.

In the second passage, Paul tells us he disregards the failures and mistakes of his past, forgetting what is behind and pressing on. He is saying, "Whatever happened to you yesterday, whatever loss you endured, press on regardless." It's one of the best responses to the unexpected.

Could it be that disappointment is actually a grace? How can this be? When I am disappointed in my circumstances or in other people, the pain of that moment leads me to trust the only One who can truly satisfy the longings and dreams in my soul. And with that trust arises faith. And when my faith brings me to the place where I believe no matter what my situation that God's love for me is perfect

A sweet friendship refreshes the soul. PROVERBS 27:9

Scripture quotations from The Message. © Eugene Peterson. Permission from Navpress

38911

© DAYSPRING CARDS
SILOAM SPRINGS
ARKANSAS
MADE IN CHINA

In my
prayers

Dearest J—

You are such a blessing
to me — to so many!

I love you —

God Bless you —

always —

and His wisdom is infallible, my disappointment fades away. The Scriptures affirm this: "Whoever believes in Him will not be disappointed" (Romans 10:11 NASB).

THE GRACE OF AFFLICTION

Keep this in mind: We don't always know why God allows problems, but we know He intends to use them to heighten our maturity and deepen our faith. Trials and troubles are dumbbells and treadmills for the soul. They develop strength and stamina. His Word says:

> Many are the afflictions of the righteous,
> but the LORD delivers him out of them all
> (Psalm 34:19 NASB).

> Call upon Me in the day of trouble;
> I will deliver you, and you shall glorify Me
> (Psalm 50:15 NKJV).

> The Lord will deliver me from every evil work and preserve me for His heavenly kingdom. To Him be glory forever (2 Timothy 4:18 NKJV).

Is it possible there is *comfort in suffering*? Are there any kinds of benefits?

Can we become all that God wants us to be without affliction? The Bible indicates that the answer is no. We really need the grace of affliction. It's true, trials and tribulations are painful at the time, and we should never seek them out. Yet when they come, they come as God's grace to help us grow, mature, and stay on the right path. David understood that affliction is actually a blessing. How is it good? How does this help us obey? How are God's laws righteous?

It was good for me to be afflicted
　　so that I might learn your decrees…
Before I was afflicted I went astray,
　　but now I obey your word…
I know, Lord, that your laws are righteous,
　　and that in faithfulness you have afflicted me…
If your law had not been my delight,
　　I would have perished in my affliction
　　　　　　　　　　　　(Psalm 119:71,67,75,92).

It's true that once a crisis hits, your life will never be exactly the way it was.

These events are like bombs that spray their lethal projectiles all around without regard for anyone standing in the way. The haunting words of an old children's game reflect the fallout of a crisis.

Ring around the rosy,
Pocketful of posies
Ashes, ashes,
All fall down.

But if we let Him, God uses the fallout from these events to refine and hone the sense of His love toward us and His sovereignty in our lives. But when you're in the midst of dealing with a trauma, that's not what you want to hear.

These events will either destroy us or transform us. Survivors are the ones who understand the typical ways of responding to these events and the stages they will experience as they walk through it.

Some individuals may not wrestle with questions about God's existence, but trauma commonly produces questions about God's nature or character. Following a traumatic event, survivors will ask such questions as, "Is God really good?" "Does God care about what I'm going through?" "Is God taking care of me?" "Why do bad things happen?" All of these questions have to do with God's character, what God is like…

While anger can be expressed at many different targets, individuals often feel anger toward God…

Following trauma, a person may discover that he or she is having difficulties with common religious practices such as prayer, Bible reading, or attendance of religious services or activities. Even a devoted believer may notice a lack of desire for religious matters. Often, this lack of desire for familiar religious expressions produces guilt, compounding matters. Some individuals may experience a lack of desire for religious expressions, but may note frustration or impatience with religious expressions that seem shallow or simplistic. Some believers find themselves feeling alienated from their religious traditions or from their regular places of worship…

It's not unusual for survivors to pull away from significant relationships, even withdrawing from those who, in their past, have been their most stable sources of comfort…

Some survivors do the opposite of withdrawing from relationships; they appear to be compelled toward others. A survivor may have difficulty being alone or away from others whom they feel close to.[2]

Do you relate to this? Scott Floyd has written an excellent book on crisis counseling. This is what he said, and there is much truth in it.

1. *Being a Christian doesn't exempt us from all crises.* In some situations, God may protect someone in such a manner that he or she avoids a crisis. On other occasions, God will guide a person through a time of

crisis. All individuals, however, will experience crises, exemplified by the number and types of crises identified in Scripture. Some crisis experiences seem necessary in order to conform an individual into the image of Christ. Even the godliest individuals experience multiple crises over the course of a lifetime.

2. *A crisis to us isn't a crisis to God.* God does not panic, nor does He wring His hands, wondering what He should do next. God does not lose sleep or fret or pace the floor. What we as humans view as a crisis is not a crisis from God's vantage point. God is in control. He knows where we are and the exact nature of our circumstances. God cares about us, even in the midst of what we interpret as a crisis. [Perhaps it would help to post this point—*A crisis to us isn't a crisis to God*—on a poster and read it over each day until it's embedded in your mind.]

3. *God comforts and promises to be present.* I'm amazed at how many times God encourages His children to "Fear not," often adding the assurance, "I am with you." Many of the most godly biblical figures received reassurance of God's care and presence when they faced crises: Abraham (Gen. 15:1), Jacob (Gen. 26:24), Moses (Num. 21:34), Joshua (Josh. 8:1), Gideon (Judg. 6:23), Solomon (1 Chron. 28:20), Jeremiah (Lam. 3:27), Daniel (Dan. 10:12), Zechariah (Luke 1:13), Joseph (Matt. 1:20), Mary (Luke 1:30), Peter (Luke 5:10), Paul (Acts 27:24), and John (Rev. 1:17). God cares for His children, provides words of comfort and promises to be present in difficult circumstances. Go back and read each passage.

4. *A crisis will not last forever.* One of my favorite phrases in the Bible is "And it came to pass…" Our timing

is not the same as God's timing. God knows what we need and when we need it. Even difficult circumstances will eventually change or God will provide us strength to face and cope with the crisis.

5. *Hope is resident in crises.* Paul understood that crises do not have to end in hopelessness and despair. In Romans 5:3-5, Paul acknowledges that believers will have struggles, but difficult times do not have to dictate negative outcomes: "But we also exult in our tribulations, knowing that tribulation brings about perseverance; and perseverance, proven character and proven character, hope; and hope does not disappoint, because the love of God has been poured out within our hearts through the Holy Spirit who was given to us." Difficult circumstances have the ability to produced perseverance, character, and hope. It is, in fact, this hope that helps us look ahead, to face the crises that are so much a part of life in this world.[3]

The specific word *crisis* does not appear in Scriptures, but the Bible contains many accounts of crises. Such include unstable time periods or turning points in the lives of biblical figures. We do find in Scripture terms that parallel crisis—*trial, tribulation, test, persecution,* and *affliction.*

These terms seem to be common components of what all humans experience in life, even believers who are attempting to follow Christ. In 1 Peter 4:12, for example, Peter tells believers to "not be surprised at the painful trial you are suffering, as though something strange were happening to you" (NIV). James encourages followers to: "Consider it all joy, my brethren, when you encounter various trials" (James 1:2). Just prior to the crucifixion, Jesus informs His disciples, "In the world you have tribulation, but take courage: I have overcome the world" (John 16:33). In the Old Testament, Genesis 22:2, God tests Abraham by asking him to sacrifice his son, Isaac. God, in Deuteronomy 8:2, tells the children of Israel that He led them into the wilderness to humble them and to test them. This testing involved allowing them to be hungry (Deut. 8:3, 16), thirsty (Deut. 8:15), and in physical danger (Deut. 8:15). Paul informs the Thessalonians that "when we were with you, we kept telling you in advance that we were going to suffer affliction; and so it came to pass, as you know" (1 Thess. 3:4). Individuals in Scriptures were no stranger to crises.

Other terms, too, used in Scripture are similar to crisis, including *suffering*, *hardship*, *adversity*, and *pain*. In Romans 5:3, Paul says, "We also rejoice in our sufferings, because we know that suffering produces perseverance" (NIV). Jesus also experienced suffering, telling His followers, "the Son of Man must suffer many things" (Mark 8:31). Peter states, "To this you were called, because Christ suffered for you, leaving you an example, that you should follow in his steps."[4]

UNEXPECTED EVENTS ARE NOT UNIQUE

Unexpected events are not unique to our time. Even in Jesus's day, people experienced devastation that sounds similar to that of the present day. Luke records a brief interaction between Jesus and some of His followers (Luke 13:1-5). They discussed a political murder for which Pilate was responsible—a group of worshippers were killed while they were in the process of making their sacrifices. In the same conversation, Jesus mentioned 18 individuals killed in Siloam when a tower fell on them.

Two tragic events—one the murder of individuals involved in a religious ceremony, and the other a terrible accident with multiple victims. Jesus's listeners seemed familiar with the second event; perhaps people in the surrounding countryside had been talking, as we do today, about what had happened and why. When His followers questioned Jesus, He used these events to point them to God and to His larger purposes.

We have always had to contend with natural disasters—earthquakes, volcanoes, fires, floods, famines, tornadoes, and hurricanes. Not only that, we have also been responsible for some of their own disasters, including building collapses, fires, plane crashes, and ships sinking. Throughout the centuries, we've experienced terrorist attacks, wars, and other aggressive acts, producing unbelievable loss of lives. Diseases, such as bubonic plague, influenza, plagues, tuberculosis, and small pox, have killed millions.

Crises and traumatic events have been a part of human experience since creation.[5] Each age has, indeed, had its own set of difficulties. This past year has produced the worst terrorist attacks and the worst fires on record.

Here is what James Dobson has to say:

> If you are suffering because of disillusionment or confusion, I am writing with you in mind. I know you are hurting. I understand the pain that engulfed you when your child died or your husband betrayed you or your beloved wife went to be with Jesus. You could not explain the devastating earthquake, or the fire, or the terrible tornado, or the unreasonable rainstorm that ruined your crops. The insurance company said it was an "act of God." Yes. That's what hurt most.[6]

The natural reaction is to say, "Lord, is *this* the way You treat Your own? I thought You cared for me, but I was wrong. I can't love a God like that." It's a tragic misunderstanding.

Scripture is replete with examples of this troubling human experience. Moses, for instance, in his appeal to Pharaoh for the release of the children of Israel, had good reason to feel God had pushed him out on a limb and abandoned him there. He reacted as you or I would under the circumstances: "LORD, why have you brought trouble upon this people? Is this why you sent me?" (Exodus 5:22).

The great danger for people who have experienced this kind of tragedy is that Satan will use their pain to make them feel victimized by God. What a deadly trap that is! When a person begins to conclude that he or she is disliked or hated by the Almighty, demoralization is not far behind.

TRUSTING THE WISDOM OF GOD

For the heartsick, bleeding soul out there today who is desperate for a word of encouragement, let me assure you that you can trust the Lord of heaven and earth. There is security and rest in the wisdom of the eternal God. The Lord can be trusted—even when He can't be tracked. Of this you can be certain: Jehovah, the King of kings and Lord of lords, is not pacing the corridors of heaven in confusion over the problems in your life! He hung the worlds in space. He can handle the burdens that have weighed you down, and He cares about you deeply.

Our view of God is too small—His power and His wisdom cannot even be imagined by us mortals. He is not just "the man upstairs" or "the great chauffeur in the sky" or some kind of wizard who will do a dance for those who make the right noises.

If we truly understood the majesty of the Lord and the depth of His love for us, we would certainly accept those times when He defies human logic and sensibilities. Indeed, that is what we must do. Expect confusing experiences to occur along the way. Welcome them as friends—as opportunities for your faith to grow. Hold fast to your faith, without which it is impossible to please Him. Never let yourself succumb to the notion to that God has somehow betrayed you. Instead, store away your questions in a file under the heading "Things I Don't Understand," and leave them there—and be thankful that God does what is best for us whether or not it conforms to our wishes.[7]

Pastor and author Warren Wiersbe writes, "Quite frankly, there are no explanations for some of the things which happen in life; nor are we required to devise any. People need God more than they need explanation."[8]

The central challenge for us lies not in explaining suffering but rather in facing it and making it a witness *for* God rather than *against* God.[9] When we embrace an image of God as all-powerful, we turn to God in times of trouble. What can God, in the face of such reality, do for us?

I've thought much about the following statement as I've heard the stories of trauma from so many: "To see the face of God in trauma requires that sometimes we visit places where we would prefer not to go. One of the most difficult passages is recognition of the poverty of our images of God to explain the mystery of suffering, take it away, or at times, even offer much in the way of comfort."[10]

Warren Wiersbe suggests there are four gifts that come from God. *First*, we are given courage in our faith to face life honestly. We do not have to run away from the horror or become bitter in its wake. Instead, we accept the tension that the downside of happiness is sorrow and the joy of life its burden. That is the way life is. *Second*, God gives us wisdom, in time, to understand what needs to be done. This direction comes through prayer and an openness to God's healing spirit. A *third* gift is the strength to do what must be done. Almost all of us who have lived through trauma look back in amazement at what God allowed us to do in the moment. *Finally*, God gives us faith to be patient. God can work even through the brokenness to bring good into the world.[11]

CHAPTER 12

You Can Live Fear-Free

And so we come to the conclusion of this book. There is just one more subject to be addressed. It's a four-letter word...*fear*. It's the result and residue of the presence of an unexpected event or trauma.

You and I have the potential to develop unreasonable fears. And most come from our life experiences, especially trauma. The abundance of fears is overwhelming. I've heard about so many from those who have experienced the shooting at Las Vegas. The fear of what might be in that backpack or briefcase or the sounds of a crowd or a book dropped or a loud voice or the smell of smoke or a bright light in a window. You and I were born with the capability of becoming afraid, and fear is useful and normal—but it can also get out of hand. When fear is generated from the unexpected or unthinkable, it usually goes over the edge!

Fear can drive us, and it can freeze us. Our bodies can tremble with the aftermath of fear. Some fears turn into phobias that are more irrational because they don't respond or go away logically.

Fear is a glaring red light on the highway of risk and change. As one person said, "Fear was in my driver's seat and it was taking me for a ride." Fear disables. Fear cripples. Fear clouds our vision. Fear shortens life. Fear cripples our relationship with others. Fear blocks our relationship with God. Fear keeps us from experiencing the blessings of God because it short-circuits our choices and keeps us from change.

Fear can cause us to imagine the worst possible outcome of our efforts.

Fear can limit the development of various alternatives and put the brakes on moving forward during times of chaos!

The cry of those who have experienced the unexpected is, "I don't feel safe!" It's as though a masked bandit invaded our personal life and ripped away what we need to survive. What this robbery accomplished permeated every aspect of our life; it not only took something away, it left something in its place—fear.

It permeates and dominates our life. Can you recover? Yes. Is it easy? Not necessarily. Does it take time? Yes.

What do we know about fear? It can make us more alert. It can warn us so it's constructive. But it can cause us to overreact, which means it can mislead us. I've seen so much of this after an accident or a shooting. It's been suggested that our fear has actually made terrorist threats more effective than they would otherwise be.[1]

Most in our country are looking for a risk-free environment, and perhaps what we need to do is learn to live with the reality there will always be unexpected events. Scripture does not teach freedom from risk but how to handle the difficulties. We can't live risk-free, but we can learn to live fear-free. That's the promise of God's Word. And keep in mind that some fears are desirable if they make us more alert.

What do we know about fear? It can worsen the quality of life. When you live with fear, it takes the edge off the enjoyment of life. We have a desire for security as well as the desire for feeling safe. But as was said before—fear erodes feeling safe.

And when excessive fear exists, it distorts. We assume the worst and think the worst. It's like taking a balloon with the word *fear* written on it. When it is blown up according to a certain size and no further, it lasts and is pliable. But blowing it up with no regard to the instructions can lead to the demise of the existence of the balloon.

Excessive fear can lead not only to wrong decisions but sometimes to measures that are counterproductive.

This kind of fear can cause us to make decisions based more on emotion than on fact. An example of this is some of the travel restrictions against certain ethnic groups.

Sometimes our fear can distort our focus, and we give too much attention to one fear at the expense of doing something about others that are legitimate concerns.

Our concern in this chapter is the everyday fear, which is left over from the events that rips away a person's sense of safety.

There are certain responses that generate anxiety as well as fear. Consider whether that is how you respond and look at your life. We avoid what we fear. One person said, "Face the fear and do it anyway." Many of us have learned patterns of avoidance. If you want your fear and anxiety to flourish, avoid it even if something upsetting has destroyed your feeling of safety. Avoidance accomplishes what you don't want. It's better to expose yourself. Experience is the solution, as strange as it seems.

So, what are the types of avoidance that will increase fear and anxiety? One is escape behavior. This includes anything you do in the heat of the moment. Running from what you fear is a classic example. The more you do this, the more your tolerance decreases.

Another response is avoidant behavior. These are the things you do to stay away from anxiety-producing experiences. You make a decision, right or wrong, and anxiety wins out so you avoid the situation.

A third response is procrastination—you put something off because you're sure it will create anxiety. You convince yourself this will not be a good idea. You rationalize that this is the best idea.

Safety behavior involves doing things to give you a sense of safety. Sometimes you distract yourself so you feel more comfortable. It allows you to remain present, but some of your behavior becomes stressful or a nervous habit.[2]

Because avoidance results in temporary reduction of fear, it serves as a powerful short-term reinforcer. It is therefore difficult to resist. The more you avoid what makes you anxious, the more elaborate the forms of avoidance can become. If avoidance takes the extreme, you can even become agoraphobic, afraid to leave your home. Once you begin avoiding, it's difficult to stop.

Avoidance is difficult to avoid for the following reasons:

- It works to reduce fear for a short amount of time.

- The more you engage in avoidance, the harder it is to resist engaging in it in the future because it becomes a habit.

- There is superficial logic to avoidance, such as, "Why wouldn't I avoid something that makes me anxious?"

- You get a secondary gain from it, like extra care, because people around you are sympathetic.

By engaging in avoidance, you stir up the "worry circuit" in the brain. The worry circuit stirs up the alarm section, which increases your sense of fear, and the overactivity of the alarm tries to figure out why you feel anxious. The extreme version of the worry circuit occurs with people who suffer from OCD, a condition in which the worries become obsessive.[3]

Worry is the fear we manufacture—it is not authentic. If you choose to worry about something, have at it, but do so knowing it's a choice. Most often, we worry because it provides some secondary reward. There are many variations, but a few of the most popular follow.

- Worry is a way to avoid change; when we worry we don't do anything about the matter.

- Worry is a way to avoid admitting powerlessness over something, since worry feels like we're doing something.

When you feel fear, listen.

When you don't feel fear, don't manufacture it.

If you find yourself creating worry, explore and discover why.[4]

Fear internalized grows in power over us, and our sense of safety shrinks. As we agree with fear, it's like we are saying it's true. Fear plays movies in our head of imagined outcomes of worst-case scenarios that are not true. The design of fear is to rob us of our courage and to stop us in our tracks, even cause us to retreat. That was what the enemy of America intended to do; that is also what the enemy of our souls intends to do. That is one reason we should not give in to fear...

One of the mightiest weapons in our arsenal against fear is the remembrance, remembrance of God's faithfulness. God knows that we tend to forget.[5]

We were created in God's image to represent Him to people. Like a blanket, fear covers over the image of God in us. If we hide under the cover of fear, we hide ourselves from the very things we were created to do and be.[6]

We can live fear-free—let's remember that.

Appendix: Resources for Help

A.L.I.C.E. #1 ACTIVE SHOOTER RESPONSE TRAINING FOR ALL ORGANIZATIONS

ALICE (Alert, Lockdown, Inform, Counter, Evacuate)—Training-instructor-led classes provide preparation and a plan for individuals and organizations on how to more proactively handle the threat of an aggressive intruder or active shooter event. Whether it is an attack by an individual person or by an international group of professionals intent on conveying a political message through violence, ALICE Training option-based tactics have become the accepted response, versus the traditional "lockdown only" approach. Provides training for police/law enforcement, K-12 schools, healthcare, higher education, business, government, houses of worship.

www.alicetraining.com/

AMERICAN PSYCHOLOGICAL ASSOCIATION

Article: "Managing Your Stress After a Shooting"—www.apa.org/helpcenter/mass-shooting.aspx

AMERICAN RED CROSS

Article: "Preparation Before and After Terrorist Attacks"—www
.redcross.org/get-help/how-to-prepare-for-emergencies/types
-of-emergencies/terrorism

1-800 HELP NOW; www.redcross.org

CDC INJURY PREVENTION

Article: "Coping with a Traumatic Event"—www.cdc.gov/masstrauma
/factsheets/public/coping.pdf

FEDERAL EMERGENCY MANAGEMENT AGENCY (FEMA)

1(800) 462-9092; www.fema.gov

OFFICE FOR VICTIMS OF CRIMES

www.ovc.gov/help/domestic_terrorism.html

HOMELAND SECURITY

Article: "Preventing Terrorism"—https://www.dhs.gov/preventing
-terrorism

NASP

Article: "Helping Children Cope with Terrorism—Tips for Families
and Educators"—www.nasponline.org/resources-and-publications
/resources/school-safety-and-crisis/war-and-terrorism/helping
-children-cope-with-terrorism

NATIONAL ORGANIZATION FOR VICTIMS ASSISTANCE

1730 Park Rd, NW
Washington, DC 20010

1(800)TRY-NOVA

OPTUM

Article: "Responding to Traumatic Events in the Workplace"—
www.optum.com/content/dam/optum/resources/whitePapers
/5218_CIRS_White_Paper08062014.pdf

Notes

CHAPTER 1—TREMORS IN OUR LIFE

1. Alice E. Robertson, *Blindsided: Lessons from Job on Surviving Your Trauma* (North Charleston, SC: Booksurge Publishing, 2005), introduction.

2. Amanda Ripley, *The Unthinkable: Who Survives When Disaster Strikes—and Why* (New York: Three Rivers Press, 2009), adapted, 38.

3. Fiona Marshall, *Losing a Parent* (Cambridge Center, MA: Fisher Books, 1993), 45.

4. Ripley, adapted, xvi-xvii.

5. M.J. Ryan, *How to Survive Change You Don't Ask For* (Newburyport, MA: Conari Press, 2014), adapted, 3-4.

6. Ryan, 10.

7. Steven Fink, *Crisis Management: Planning for the Inevitable* (Vancouver, BC: Amacom, 1986), 37.

8. Fink, adapted, 37.

9. Sharon Begley, *Train Your Mind, Change Your Brain* (New York: Ballantine Books, 2007).

CHAPTER 2—THE UNEXPECTED—INEVITABLE

1. H. Norman Wright, *When the Past Won't Let You Go* (Eugene, OR: Harvest House, 2016), 9-11.

2. Amanda Ripley, *The Unthinkable: Who Survives When Disaster Strikes—and Why* (New York: Three Rivers Press, 2009), adapted, 230-232.

3. Max Lucado, *In the Eye of the Storm* (Dallas: Word, 1991), 105-106.

4. Robert Hicks, *Failure to Scream* (Nashville, TN: Thomas Nelson, 1993), 172.

5. Lewis Smedes, *How Can It Be All Right When Everything Is All Wrong?* (San Francisco: Harper & Row, 1982), 55-56.

6. Barry Johnson, *Choosing Hope* (Nashville, TN: Abingdon, 1988), 178.

CHAPTER 4—BOUNCING BACK

1. Dave Dravecky with Tim Stafford, *Comeback* (Grand Rapids, MI: Zondervan, 1990), adapted, 16.

2. Langston Hughes, as quoted in Ann Kaiser Stearns, *Living Through Personal Crisis* (Chicago: Thomas Moore, 1984), 25.

3. Marilyn Willett Heavelin, *When Your Dreams Die* (San Bernardino, CA: Here's Life, 1990), 30-31.

4. Ann Stearns, *Coming Back* (New York: Random House, 1988), adapted, 218-219.

5. Charles Figley, *Trauma and Its Wake* (Levittown, PA: Brunner/Mazel, 1985), xviii.

6. Robert Hicks, *Failure to Scream* (Nashville, TN: Thomas Nelson, 1993), 13, 15.

CHAPTER 5—THE PHASES—THEY'RE NORMAL

1. Ann Stearns, *Coming Back* (New York: Random House, 1988), 85-86.

2. Amanda Ripley, *The Unthinkable: Who Survives When Disaster Strikes—and Why* (New York: Three Rivers Press, 2009), adapted, 38.

3. Ripley, adapted, xvi-xvii.

4. Ripley, 38-39, 58.

5. Ripley, 91.

6. Ripley, 220-221.

7. Robert Hicks, *Failure to Scream* (Nashville, TN: Thomas Nelson, 1993), adapted, 46.

8. Aaron Lazare et al, "The Walk-In Patient as a 'Customer': A Key Dimension in Evaluation and Treatment," *American Journal of Orthopsychiatry* 42, 1979, 872-883.

9. Max Lucado, *Eye of the Storm* (Dallas: Word, 1991), adapted, 193-194.

10. William Pruitt, *Run from the Pale Pony* (Grand Rapids, MI: Baker, 1976), 9-10.

CHAPTER 6—YOUR BRAIN: TREAT IT WELL

1. Amit Sood, MD, *The Mayo Clinic Guide to Stress-Free Living* (Burlington, VT: Da Capo, 2013), 2.

2. Heather Davediuk Gingrich, PhD, *Restoring the Shattered Self: A Christian Counselor's Guide to Complex Trauma* (Downers Grove, IL: IVP Academic, 2013), adapted, 38-39.

3. Bessel van der Kolk, *The Body Keeps Score: Brain, Mind and Body in the Healing of Trauma* (New York: Penguin Books, 2015), adapted, 44.

4. Judith Herman, *Trauma and Recovery* (New York: Basic Books, 1982), adapted, 42-43.

5. Van der Kolk, 52.

6. M.J. Ryan, *How to Survive Change You Didn't Ask For* (Newburyport, MA: Conari Press, 2014), adapted. 22.

7. Ryan, *How to Survive Change You Didn't Ask For,* adapted, 20, 22-23.

8. John B. Arden, *Rewire Your Brain: Think Your Way to a Better Life* (Hoboken, NJ: Wiley Publishing, 2010), adapted, 43-44.

9. Dr. Dave Ziegler, *Beyond Healing* (Phoenix, AZ: Acacia Publications, 2009), adapted, 98-192.

10. David J. Morris, *The Evil Hours* (Chicago: Eamon Dolan/Mariner Books, 2016), adapted, 47.

11. Van der Kolk, adapted, 44-45.

12. Herman, adapted, 47.

13. Van der Kolk, adapted, 60.

14. Babette Rothschild, *The Body Remembers* (New York: W.W. Norton, 2000), adapted, 12.

15. Ryan, adapted, 4, 5, 10.

16. Ryan, adapted, 28-29.

17. Ryan, adapted, 57.

18. Ryan, 70.

19. Jennifer Cisney and Kevin Ehlers, *The First 48 Hours* (Nashville, TN: Abingdon Press, 2009), adapted, 29.

20. Laurence Gonzales, *Surviving Survival* (New York: W.W. Norton & Company, 2013), adapted, 29.

21. Sharon Begley, *Train Your Mind, Change Your Brain* (New York: Ballantine Books, 2007), 8.

22. John Selby, *Quiet Your Mind* (Novato, CA: New World Library, 2004), 40-41.

23. Melanie Greenberg, PhD, *The Stress-Proof Brain* (Oakland, CA: New Harbinger, 2017), 65.

24. Greenberg, adapted, 60, 61 and 3.

25. Greenberg, adapted, 3-4.

26. Greenberg, adapted, 17.

27. Aphrodite Matsakis, PhD, *Trust After Trauma* (Oakland, CA: New Harbinger, 1988), adapted, 9-10.

28. Matsakis, 105.

29. Aaron Fruh, *Bounce* (Ada, MI: Baker Publishing Group, 2017), adapted, 20-21.

CHAPTER 7—TERRORISM

1. Amanda Ripley, *The Unthinkable: Who Survives When Disaster Strikes—and Why* (New York: Three Rivers Press, 2009), adapted, 32.

2. Jeffrey D. Simon, *Lone Wolf Terrorism: Understanding the Growing Threat* (Amherst, NY: Prometheus Books, 2016), adapted, 181.

3. Jeffrey D. Simon, *The Terrorist Trap: America's Experience with Terrorism* (Bloomington, IN: Indiana University Press, 2001), 5.

4. Simon, *The Terrorist Trap*, 344-345.

5. Simon, *The Terrorist Trap*, adapted, 9-10.

6. Martha Crenshaw and Gary LaFree, *Countering Terrorism* (Washington, DC: Brookings Institution Press, 2017), 44-45.

7. Crenshaw and LaFree, adapted, 35-36.

8. Compilation based on Global Terrorism Database; http://www.start.umd.edu/gtd/.

9. Tore Bjorgo, *Root Causes of Terrorism: Myths, Reality and Ways Forward* (New York: Routledge, 2005), adapted, introduction.

10. Gus Martin, *Understanding Terrorism* (Los Angeles: Sage, 2013), adapted, 165-167. Also see *A History of Christianity* by Kenneth Latourette.

11. Joshua 11 NRSV.

12. Peter Ladicola and Aaron Stupe, *Violence, Inequality and Human Freedom* (New York: General Hall, 1998), adapted, 175.

13. Martin, 165.

14. See at https://www.operation250.org/what-to-talk-about/, adapted.

15. Martin, adapted, 35-37.

16. Jessica Hamblen, PhD, and Laurie B. Sloane, PhD, http://www.westga.edu/~vickir/PublicSafety/PS05%20Training%20and%20Education/PS05situational_factors.pdf, adapted.

17. Amy Zalman, PhD, https://www.thoughtco.com/the-causes-of-terrorism-3209053, September 25, 2017, adapted.

18. Simon, *The Terrorist Trap*, 344-345.

19. Simon, *The Terrorist Trap*, adapted, 352-360.

20. Simon, *Lone Wolf Terrorism*, 242.

21. Simon, *Lone Wolf Terrorism*, adapted, 19.

22. Simon, *Lone Wolf Terrorism*, adapted, 169.

23. Simon, *Lone Wolf Terrorism*, 253.

24. Simon, *Lone Wolf Terrorism*, 29, 32.

25. Simon, *Lone Wolf Terrorism*, adapted, 43-45.

26. Simon, *Lone Wolf Terrorism*, 11.

27. Simon, *Lone Wolf Terrorism*, 232.

28. Simon, *The Terrorist Trap*, vi-vii.

CHAPTER 8—TELL ME YOUR STORY

1. Robert Niemeyer, *Lessons of Loss: A Guide to Coping* (Chicago: Psychoeducational Resources, 2000), adapted, 54.

2. Brooks Brown, "Columbine Survivor with Words for Virginia Students," *All Things Considered*, NPR, air date April 18, 2007.

3. Jackson Rainer and Frieda Brown, *Crisis Counseling and Therapy* (New York: Haworth Press, 2007), adapted, 103.

4. Rainer and Brown, adapted, 105

5. Rainer and Brown, adapted, 103, 105.

6. Daniel G. Amen, *Change Your Brain, Change Your Life* (New York: Three Rivers Press, 2015), 272-273, 278-282.

7. Judith Herman, *Trauma and Recovery* (New York: Basic Books, 1992), adapted, 177.

8. Herman, adapted, 178.

9. Michael J. Scott, *Moving On After Trauma* (New York: Routledge, 2007), adapted, 64.

10. Scott, adapted, 65.

11. Scott, 72.

12. Curt Thompson, *Anatomy of the Soul* (Wheaton, IL: Tyndale House, 2010), 76.

CHAPTER 9—STEPS TO TAKE TO REGAIN CONTROL—EMOTIONS INCLUDED

1. Al Siebert, *The Resiliency Advantage* (Oakland, CA: Barrett-Koeher Publishers, 2005), adapted, 115.

2. Siebert, adapted, 107.

3. William Bridges, *The Way of Transition: Embracing Life's Most Difficult Moments* (Boston, MA: DaCapo Books, 2001), adapted, 3.

4. Andrew E. Slaby, *Aftershock* (New York: Villard Books, 1989), 39-40.

5. Judith Simon Prager and Judith Acosta, *The Worst Is Over* (San Diego, CA: Jodere Group, 2002), adapted, 278-279.

6. Theresa Rhodes McGee, *Transforming Trauma* (Maryknoll, NY: Orbis Books, 2005), 104-105.

7. Jasmin Lee Cori, *Healing from Trauma: A Survivor's Guide to Understanding Your Symptoms and Reclaiming Your Life* (Cambridge, MA: Da Capo Press, 2007), adapted 17-18.

8. Elden M. Chalmers, *Healing the Broken Brain* (Coldwater, MI: Remnant Publications, 1995), adapted, 148-149.

9. Dr. Lloyd Homme, "Thought Switching," as referenced in H. Norman Wright, *Self-Talk, Imagery and Prayer in Counseling* (Waco, TX: Word Books, 1986), 188.

CHAPTER 11—BIBLICAL VIEW OF SUFFERING

1. Andrew E. Slaby, *Aftershock* (New York: Villard Books, 1989), xii.

2. Scott Floyd, *Crisis Counseling* (Grand Rapids, MI: Kregel, 2008), 56-58.

3. Floyd, 39-40.

4. Floyd, adapted, 27-28.

5. Floyd, adapted, 15-16.

6. James Dobson, *Finding God in Perilous Times* (Wheaton, IL: 2001), 19-20.

7. Dobson, 21-22.

8. Warren Wiersbe, *When Bad Things Happen to God's People* (Old Tappan, NJ: Revell, 1984), 26.

9. Wiersbe, 115.

10. Theresa Rhodes McGee, *Transforming Trauma* (Maryknoll, NY: Orbis Books, 2005), 150.

11. Jill M. Hudson, *Congregational Trauma: Caring, Coping & Learning* (Lanham, MD: Rowman & Littlefield Publishing Co., 1998), 6-7.

CHAPTER 12—YOU CAN LIVE FEAR-FREE

1. Peter N. Stearns, *American Fear* (New York: Routledge, 2006), adapted, 201.

2. John B. Arden, *Rewire Your Brain: Think Your Way to a Better Life* (Hoboken, NJ: Wiley Publishing, 2010), adapted, 39-41.

3. Arden, adapted, 40-41.

4. Gavin de Becker, *The Gift of Fear* (New York: Dell, 1999), 302-303.

5. John Morgan, *War on Fear* (Lake Mary, FL: Creation House, 2016), 36.

6. Morgan, 62.

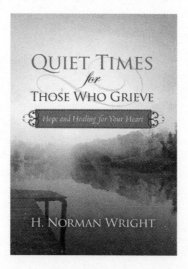

Quiet Times for Those Who Grieve

There are no words to instantly take away the deep pain of your loss. Grieving is a personal path—one that takes time to traverse. But genuine expressions of comfort and understanding can help you make gradual steps toward healing.

H. Norman Wright, a respected Christian counselor, offers these daily devotions from a heart that has endured difficult loss—yet found God faithful through it all. In these profound and practical reflections, you'll find...

- Gentle guidance through the grieving process
- Comforting reminders that you're not alone
- Hope—and the space you need to uncover it

When you're grieving, give yourself quiet moments to rest in God's limitless love and peace.

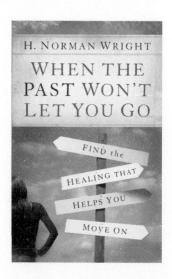

When the Past Won't Let You Go

Release your past to God once and for all with the help of respected Christian counselor H. Norman Wright, who has worked with grief-stricken individuals in the aftermath of 9/11, Hurricane Katrina, and mass shootings.

Whether you've experienced a major ordeal of a series of disappointments, it's impossible to move forward when painful emotions remain unaddressed and broken relationships stay unresolved. Reclaim hope for the future by...

- sorting through memories
- identifying lingering hurts
- overcoming former traumas
- grieving previous losses
- claiming forever freedom in Christ

Leave the past behind, experience fullness of life in the present, and look forward to the future. Healing awaits.

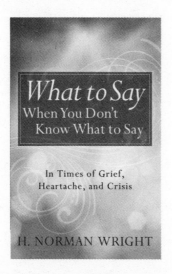

What to Say When You Don't Know What to Say

What do you do when someone says, "My mom died of cancer this morning," or "I lost my job," or "My son just announced he's getting a divorce"? When a crisis occurs, your friend needs your support. Respected counselor H. Norman Wright offers you this thorough "what to say and do" handbook packed with clear advice on how to

- respond to your friend's difficult situation
- know what help to offer and when
- assist your friend in sorting through emotions and options
- handle hard topics, including suicide and violence
- discern when more experienced help is needed

Sensitive, practical, and detailed, this straightforward guide includes what you need to be supportive and helpful—a beacon pointing to God as the ultimate healer.

To learn more about Harvest House books and
to read sample chapters, visit our website:

www.harvesthousepublishers.com

HARVEST HOUSE PUBLISHERS
EUGENE, OREGON